D0143452

The Chief Value Officer

Accountants can save the planet

CHIEF VALUE OFFICER

OFFICER

Accountants Can Save the Planet

MERVYN KING

with JILL ATKINS

Greenleaf
PUBLISHING

© 2016 Greenleaf Publishing Limited

Published by Greenleaf Publishing Limited
Salts Mill, Victoria Road, Saltaire, BD18 3LA, UK
www.greenleaf-publishing.com

The right of Mervyn King to be identified as Author of this Work has been
asserted by him in accordance with sections 77 and 78 of the Copyright,
Designs and Patents Act 1988.

Cover by Sadie Gornall-Jones

Printed and bound by CPI Group (UK) Ltd, Croydon, CR0 4YY

All rights reserved. No part of this publication may be reproduced,
stored in a retrieval system, or transmitted, in any form or by any means,
electronic, mechanical, photocopying, recording or otherwise, without
the prior permission in writing of the publishers.

British Library Cataloguing in Publication Data:
    A catalogue record for this book is available from the British Library.

    ISBN-13: 978-1-78353-296-4 [hardback]
    ISBN-13: 978-1-78353-293-3 [paperback]
    ISBN-13: 978-1-78353-295-7 [PDF ebook]
    ISBN-13: 978-1-78353-294-0 [ePub ebook]

Contents

PART II   THE DAWNING OF A NEW ERA OF CORPORATE REPORTING

PART III   VALUE CREATION AND THE CHIEF VALUE OFFICER

Figures and tables

Figures

Tables

Foreword

The term "governance", as is widely known, derives from the Latin word *gubernare* meaning "to steer". Steering a vessel across sometimes clear but often stormy seas was in the ancient world, as for sailors today, a great challenge. The art of navigating and steering a ship through whatever conditions arise carries with it grave responsibilities to the sailors on board, all senior and junior crew, the cargo, the ship itself and its owners, as well as to any other parties involved in selling or buying the wares on board or related to or affected by the ship in any manner. The safety of the ship and "all who sail in her" is very much in the hands of the captain and any senior officers.

This analogy works well for corporate governance in many ways. The training of directors, as with the training of a ship's captain and officers, is crucial not only to the success or otherwise of a company but also to the welfare of all its stakeholders including shareholders, employees, suppliers, customers, debt-holders, local communities and the natural environment with which the company interacts. The training manual, guidelines, principles and codes of best practice, and relevant regulations as well as etiquette and ethical behaviour are as important to the proper and appropriate training of boards of directors as to that of seafaring captains.

This book encapsulates not only a complete and comprehensive guide for 21st-century directors, accountants and indeed all involved in corporate governance but also provides a framework for best practice that far exceeds the minimum standard required.

Most of the concepts arise from the four successive "King Reports" on South African corporate governance (King Committee on Corporate Governance, 1994, 2002, 2009). In my view (and I am sure that of many other academics and practitioners) the first King Report was revolutionary and radical in its approach and scope. In 1994 when King I was published, the only explicit national code of practice already in existence was the Cadbury Code and its accompanying Cadbury Report (Corporate Governance Committee, 1992). This corporate governance code was essentially shareholder-centric, with the radical element being the first attempt to bring shareholder activism and institutional investor engagement and dialogue into the core of governance. The first King Report (which I remember receiving in hard copy with great excitement) was completely different. Indeed, King I included a code of business ethics for stakeholders and companies. King II, published in 2002, went even further. For me, one of the most important elements of King II was the distinction drawn between "accountability" and "responsibility", as follows,

> One is liable to render an account when one is accountable and one is liable to be called to account when one is responsible. In governance terms, one is accountable at common law and by statute to the company if a director and one is responsible to the stakeholders identified as relevant to the business of the company. The stakeholder concept of being accountable to all legitimate stakeholders must be rejected for the simple reason that to ask boards to be accountable to everyone would result in their being accountable to no one. The modern approach is

> for a board to identify the company's stakeholders, including
> its shareowners, and to agree policies as to how the relationship
> with those stakeholders should be advanced and managed in
> the interests of the company (King Committee, 2002, p. 5).

Fourteen years on, and two further King Reports later, this is still an important notion for a corporate governance that embeds stakeholder responsibility at its core. King III, published in 2009, further emphasized the need for companies to act responsibly towards their stakeholders and introduced the concept of holistic governance. As is well documented, the most significant outcome of King III was the introduction of (effectively) mandatory integrated reporting in South Africa. As we shall see in this book, integrated reporting has substantially altered the way in which companies in South Africa report on social, ethical and environmental issues as well as the way they embed these factors within their strategic business plan through integrated thinking. Integrated reporting is already making inroads globally, with leading companies around the world adopting integrated reporting, if not by name, by content and approach.

It is chiefly the King Reports that led me to develop my own definition of corporate governance, which encapsulates all of these essential stakeholder-oriented approaches to governance, such that corporate governance is, "the system of checks and balances, both internal and external to companies, which ensures that companies discharge their accountability to all their stakeholders and act in a socially responsible way in all areas of their business activity" (Solomon, 2013, p. 7).

Certainly, it seems that the essence of corporate governance is the specific checks, balances or "mechanisms" that ensure that companies behave in a responsible manner *vis-à-vis* stakeholders, society at large and the natural environment, as well as discharging accountability, or rather responsibility in King's terms, to their shareholders. I have often wondered why South Africa was the birthplace of truly stakeholder-inclusive governance. Perhaps it is the complex political environment, the massive income inequalities, poverty and social challenges, or the rich and world-famous ecology and biodiversity. I have come to the conclusion that it is a combination of all of these and one other magical ingredient: Mervyn King. Indeed, this is the case with many great changes in governance and accountability—an inspirational voice, or a social activist, tends to play a transformative role. The late Sir Adrian Cadbury in UK governance and James Gifford for his role in creating the Principles of Responsible Investment are just two other such.

This book brings together a whole range of mechanisms critical to attaining a corporate governance that enhances value for shareholder and stakeholders, for the company, while at the same time enhancing societal welfare. They are also mechanisms that can, if properly applied, avert ecological disaster and literally "save the planet". A company that genuinely, and in good faith, incorporates integrated reporting, integrated thinking, an effective chief value officer, the appropriate chief stakeholder relations officer and principles of corporate governance (King IV naturally) should produce a virtuous circle of growth, value creation, stakeholder satisfaction, enhanced societal welfare and proper environmental stewardship.

The concept of integrated reporting represents a sea change in the function of accounting and reporting. Narrative (and increasingly quantitative and financial) reporting on a company's impact on biodiversity, on local communities, on employees' welfare and safety, on carbon footprint and on ecological impacts, to name but a few, are critically important elements to a fully functioning integrated report. The process of integrated thinking that must underlie integrated reporting needs to incorporate all of these issues as material financial matters, as factors affecting corporate strategy and as components of value creation. Companies that refuse to recognize and acknowledge the crucial relevance of this will fail as we move further into the 21st century. Extinction accounting, a new concept discussed in this book, represents one way in which corporate reporting and especially integrated reporting can "save the planet". Similarly, the role of the chief value officer and the chief stakeholder relations officer, if carried out as suggested in this book, can, and hopefully will, "save the planet".

Professor King's contribution to governance is a shining light in a corporate world that can often be dark and brooding, frequently beset with corporate scandals, unethical practices, bribery, corruption, maltreatment of employees and environmental degradation. If we see governance as the steering of a ship then this book and the robust, far-reaching framework proposed within, is a lighthouse, standing out in the most dangerous waters, which guides, warns, advises and protects companies and their stakeholders. Accounting has often been seen as a means of shedding light and illuminating corporate activity. This book provides a means of ensuring that corporate accounting and accountability not only shed light but enlighten and enrich corporate dialogue with stakeholders, bringing with it the warm glow of corporate responsibility, sustainability and enhanced societal welfare. Taking heed of a lighthouse ensures safety of the crew, the ship, all parties involved in its sailing and safety and protects the natural environment for the benefit of future generations.

Professor Jill Atkins
University of Sheffield
September 201

Prologue

The purpose of this book is to explore a number of propositions and provide evidence for why they are "true". First, we question whether shareholders are actually the owners of a company and come to the conclusion that despite traditional finance theory, they are not. There is a discussion of traditional, orthodox shareholder-centric models of governance. This discussion leads to the conclusion that they are no longer fit for purpose in today's world. Further, there is a need to change to an inclusive stakeholder-centric governance model where directors discharge their duties in the best interests of the company but give parity to the sources of value creation, which includes the ongoing relationship between the company and its material stakeholders. Indeed, this book asserts that a shareholder-centric model based on the primacy of the shareholder, or even the concept of the "enlightened shareholder", is not a governance approach that will change corporate behaviour to one that will lead to value creation in a sustainable manner. Our climate is in crisis, nature is in crisis and populations are threatened by global warming. A shareholder-centric approach will not deal with these global catastrophic issues.

Accounting and finance has to change at its very essence. The finance professional today should not only prepare the financial statements according to financial reporting standards; the finance professional has a critical role to play in the change from maximising profits for shareholders to maintaining value creation in a sustainable manner. His or her role is more of a value officer than a financial officer. Consequently, the CFO (chief financial officer) should be known as the CVO—the chief value officer. This concept is absolutely essential and needs to be implemented in companies around the world to ensure value creation that is in line with sustainability goals and targets such as carbon emissions targets.

If accountants are going to be able to contribute to saving the planet, and in fact lead other professions, the way in which they are educated and trained needs to undergo a seismic change. It is essential that the training and education of those entering the accountancy profession is transformed to embrace the changed thinking in value creation in a sustainable manner as opposed to profit-making for shareholders even at a cost to society or the environment. This alteration involves ensuring that accountants and financial managers are incorporated into integrated thinking, and that they learn how to produce truly integrated reports. In summary, it is in the long-term best interests of shareholders for a board to give parity to the sources of value creation, which implies the primacy of sustainable development in all business strategies and in corporate reporting.

Abbreviations

ACCA	Association of Chartered & Certified Accountants
A4S	The Prince's Accounting for Sustainability
AICPA	American Institute of Certified Public Accountants
CDSB	Climate Disclosure Standards Board
CEO	chief executive officer
CFO	chief financial officer
COO	chief operating officer
CSEAR	Centre for Social and Environmental Accounting Research
CSR	corporate social responsibility
CSRO	chief stakeholder relations officer
CVO	**chief value officer**
ESG	environmental, social and governance
FASB	Financial Accounting Standards Board
GAAP	Generally Accepted Accounting Principles
GRI	Global Reporting Initiative
IASB	International Accounting Standards Board
ICGN	International Corporate Governance Network
IFAC	International Federation of Accountants
IFRS	International Financial Reporting Standards

IIRC	International Integrated Reporting Council
IMF	International Monetary Fund
IOSCO	International Organisation for Securities Commissions
IPO	initial public offering
ISAR	International Standards of Accounting and Reporting
IUCN	International Union for Conservation of Nature
OFR	Operating and Financial Review
PRI	Principles of Responsible Investment
SASB	Sustainability Accounting Standards Board
SDGs	Sustainable Development Goals
SEC	Securities and Exchange Commission
UN	United Nations
UNCBD	United Nations Convention on Biological Diversity
UNCTAD	United Nations Conference on Trade and Development
UNEPFI	United Nations Environment Programme Finance Initiative
WWF	Worldwide Fund for Nature (previously the World Wildlife Fund)

Part I

The evolution of the corporation, directors' duties and corporate governance

In order to appreciate the challenges of ensuring effective corporate governance and accountability in today's world it is important to appreciate the way in which companies worldwide have evolved, as well as the manner in which directors' duties have changed and grown over time. This first part of the book reviews the evolution of the corporation from a historical perspective and the way corporate governance and corporate ownership structure have developed. There is then a consideration of how today's companies are, to all intents and purposes, effectively "ownerless". This part then discusses the evolution of directors' duties and the challenges faced by directors in the 21st century. Lastly, there is consideration given to the need for holistic governance and accountability.

1

The evolution of the corporation

In the 17th and 18th centuries it was a privilege to have an incorporated entity. It was done as a matter of public interest but the process was costly. The consequence was that most of the companies were unincorporated with unlimited liability to the providers of equity capital. This unlimited liability was positive for creditors but not for the development of the economy of a country. This was because wealthy families who could provide equity did not want to do it on a basis that they had unlimited liability to the providers of credit to the company or for obligations to employees. At that time, employees, on the other hand, saw the unlimited liability of the unincorporated company as a positive mechanism for secure, long-term employment. However, at the beginning of the 19th century, it was realized that from time to time the unlimited liability was in fact illusory. The shareholders did not have the means to pay the losses of the other stakeholders of the company.

Towards the middle of the 19th century, there were social and political discussions leading to pressures for the creation of a limited liability entity. The driver for this was that the wealthy middle class wanted a limitation on claims of stakeholders before investing in the equity of a company, and politicians wanted businesses to grow in order to increase jobs and stimulate the economy of a country. All this led initially in Massachusetts in America to the establishment of a limited liability company and eventually the passing of a Limited Liability Act in the United Kingdom in 1855. With the establishment of the limited liability company, directors were able to take greater risk for reward because they were able to ring-fence risk away from the providers of equity capital inside the limited liability company. This led to a clash between directors and shareholders. Shareholders wanted more control over directors.

One of the positive factors for shareholders of the limited liability company was that the shareholder had no responsibility for the liabilities of the company. At the same time there was a diminution of the incentive to avoid the bankruptcy of a company by those who were directing it. Although it was accepted that a share was no longer part of the assets of a company, there was a greater divide between the shareholders and the directors. Shareholders also accepted that the price for not being liable for any of the debts of the company was that they ranked behind the claims of all other stakeholders on bankruptcy. This led to shareholders who were supplying equity capital to a company to seek protection against any dereliction of duty by directors or excessive risk taking.

In consequence, the law developed to protect shareholders by requiring companies to disclose financial information and by giving shareholders the right to sue directors for breach of their duties of care, loyalty, good faith, skill and diligence. All these duties developed as a matter of common law, as companies became more and more the medium of choice in which business was conducted in the latter part of the 19th century and into the 20th century. All this led to the concept of the primacy of the shareholder. Directors were required to make decisions in the best interests of the general body of shareholders.

An illustration of this scenario is the famous case in the United States of America of Dodge v. Ford Motor Company in 1919. Dodge Brothers was a minority shareholder in the company. Henry Ford wanted to reinvest profits to pay Ford's employees better wages. Dodge Brothers objected to this saying that shareholders should be preferred and be paid a dividend before wages were increased. The Court ordered Ford to discharge its primary duty to shareholders and pay a special dividend to them, which included Dodge Brothers, before paying increased wages to its employees. The concept of the primacy of the shareholder and acting in the best interests of the shareholder certainly pertained well into the last quarter of the 20th century. The test of corporate success was equated with share price.

This primacy led almost naturally to the concept that shareholders were the owners of the company. At the same time, however, it was accepted that the company was sovereign and separate from its shareholders. This acceptance was core to the development of "agency theory" and a purely shareholder-oriented approach to corporate governance and accountability.

Indeed, there is an immense body of literature building on the concept of "agency theory", which is based on notions of the separation or "divorce" between shareholders and company directors. Since Berle and Means' seminal work published in 1932 identified this separation as a feature of the American pattern of corporate ownership structure prevailing at that time, agency theory and the shareholder-centric, shareholder-ownership model of governance has been the dominant discourse in corporate governance literature. Academic research, especially that arising from the US, has used the agency model as the basis for testing all aspects of corporate governance effectiveness.[1] The focus on shareholder wealth maximization and short-term shareholder satisfaction has been blamed for a whole range of corporate behaviour, including short-termism (a lack of attention to long-term strategy) and a proliferation of hostile takeover bids.

If shareholders are actually the genuine "owners" of companies then it does, to some extent at least, seem reasonable to give them some primacy. The question is, however, are they the owners? The concept that shareholders own the company turns out to be a myth.

---

1   The genesis of this extensive body of research may be found in the work of Ross (1973) and Jensen and Meckling (1976).

2

The emergence of the "ownerless company"

In 1970 the economic laureate Milton Friedman said that share-holders are "the owners of the business" and the responsibility of the corporate executive is to

> conduct the business in accordance with their designs, which generally will be to make as much money as possible while conforming to the basic rules of society... There is one and only one social responsibility of business—to use its resources and engage in activities designed to increase its profits as long as it stays in the rules of the game (Friedman 1970).

It may be doing the deceased an injustice but reading between the lines this represents a tacit statement that the company is not a part of society. Nothing could be further from the truth.

The best evidence of that today is the collapse of Lehman Brothers in 2008, which impacted adversely on a couple of billion people, and every day there is a positive impact on a few billion people aris-ing out of the developments by companies such as Microsoft and Apple. One only has to look at the wrongdoings of Robert Maxwell,

Nick Leeson, some of Enron's senior directors and other infamous cases of corporate governance failure to see how corporate collapse and unethical behaviour affects the company's pensioners, employees, local communities, taxpayers, and basically all parts of society.

Ownership has certain attributes. An owner of a "thing" is entitled to consume it, waste it or even destroy it. Shareholders have their shares, which today are in electronic form and not hard copy, but the company sits there, sovereign with its own assets and liabilities. No shareholder, be it major or minor, can use, waste or destroy any of the assets of the company. In cases where there has been a sole shareholder and that shareholder has removed moneys from the company, on bankruptcy, courts have found that the shareholder committed theft from the company. Notwithstanding the fact that the shareholder does not own the assets of the company, the shareholders have a conglomeration of very important incorporeal rights. They can decide the very purpose of the business of the company. They appoint the directors and can remove them. If the board of directors decides to pay a dividend and the company is in a financial position to pay that dividend, shareholders are entitled to receive payment of that dividend.

Analysis of shareholders of companies listed on the great stock exchanges shows that the majority of shareholders are secondary market shareholders. When a company is formed and listed on a stock exchange, people subscribe for shares in the initial public offering (IPO) by the company. Their subscriptions go into the coffers of the company. After a time those IPO shareholders sell their shares to other shareholders. It will be seen that in the second trade the money passes from the secondary market shareholder to the original IPO shareholder and does not even go into the coffers of the company.

Shareholders have a claim to a future stream of income if the company can pay its debts on due date or has readily realizable assets to pay its debts. On bankruptcy they rank behind the claims of all other creditors and stakeholders of the company. Although shareholders stand at the back of the queue they have access to self-protection. They do this by diversifying their investment in the equity of other companies. In contrast, the other stakeholders of a company such as employees or managers cannot disperse the risks they have in their contractual relationship with the company, especially on bankruptcy.

Over the years, shareholding patterns have changed substantially. In the United Kingdom the average shareholding duration in the 1960s was five years. By 2008 it was three months. Prem Sikka, Professor of Accounting at the University of Essex, points out that in computerized high-frequency trading, the average holding lasts 22 seconds! (Sikka, 2016). Prem Sikka has posed the question "What do shareholders provide to a company?" He conducted an analysis of the assets of some of the top financial institutions listed on the London Stock Exchange that shows that shareholders' funds made up a maximum of 7% of the assets of the company (see Table 2.1). Hardly a large stake in a corporation.

TABLE 2.1   **What do shareholders provide?**

Company	Year	Assets	S/H Funds	%
Barclays	2014	£1490,321	£62,957	4.22
HSBC	2014	$2,692,538	$183,129	6.8
Lloyds	2014	£924,552	£44,684	4.83
RBS	2014	£1,312,295	£70,448	5.37
Santander	2014	€1,269,628	€84,326	6.64
Std Chartered	2014	$636,518	$46,005	7.24
Prem Sikka, Essex University				

Shareholders are dispersed and transient today. The company is in fact ownerless, the same as an individual, who cannot be owned. As is well-known, slavery was abolished 180 years ago. This means that a company is like a person, at least in this characteristic.

Andrew Haldane, Chief Economist of the Bank of England, said in a speech given in 2015:

> Shareholders have... the riskiest piece of the profit pie. This means "ownership" is really a misnomer when applied to shareholders... they "own" least as residual claimants. Associating "shareholding" with "ownership" thus makes little substantive sense, despite its widespread use in popular discourse... while shareholders hold the residual risk in a company, this risk can easily be diversified away by holding a broad portfolio (Haldane, 2015).

It is to be noted that other stakeholders such as those falling under the capital rubrics of human, social, lenders, service providers etc. rank before shareholders on bankruptcy. Most companies today have their financial capital represented by loans rather than equity. The covenants of banks are stringent and many require major shareholders to cede their voting rights to the bank as collateral. In those circumstances, the most important right of a shareholder no longer exists for that shareholder, and yet in popular discourse that shareholder will continue to be called an owner of the company. Academics at universities in the United States such as Cornell, as well as Prem Sikka, have written extensively "debunking" the myth of shareholder ownership of companies.

As will be seen later in relation to inclusive governance, the move internationally is away from the shareholder-centric approach to a focus on the board applying its collective mind in the best interests of the company while giving parity to the different sources of value creation, which would include the legitimate and reasonable needs, interests and expectations of the company's material stakeholders.

In many jurisdictions the so-called "enlightened shareholder approach", as opposed to the sole primacy of the shareholder, has developed. For example, in the UK Companies Act 2006 it is stated that

> a director of a company must act in the way he considers in good faith would be most likely to promote the success of the company for the benefit of its members as a whole... but they must have regard to wider interests including employees, customers, suppliers and the wider community.

If we consider the process leading to the Companies Act 2006 it tells an interesting story of the tensions between stakeholder thinking versus shareholder thinking. The Company Law Review conducted in the UK over a number of years of consultation and debate was initiated on the understanding that directors' duties as dictated by 19th-century legislation were clearly out of date and unfit for purpose in the new millennium. Initial efforts to rewrite UK company law focused on stakeholder accountability and called for a genuinely stakeholder embedded approach to governance and accounting (see, for example, Department of Trade and Industry, 2002). Indeed, one of the most significant outcomes of the review, incorporated into the final version of company law was the mandatory Operating and Financial Review (OFR), which effectively mandated social and environmental reporting within the annual report. This was one of the first attempts, apart from the Corporate Report in the 1970s, to mandate social and environmental reporting. The eventual outcome, the Companies Act 2006, does take into account stakeholder interests but through an "enlightened shareholder" approach rather than a full-scale stakeholder-inclusive approach. In the wake of the Company Law Review process, there are mixed feelings in the business community and among those involved in the review process themselves concerning the final outcome. Some are satisfied with the enlightened shareholder approach encapsulated in the Companies Act 2006, whereas other are disappointed and had hoped to see a far more stakeholder-inclusive and pluralist approach to governance (see, for example, the findings of interviews with those involved in the review process in Collison *et al.*, 2011). However, it is worth emphasizing that the Companies Act 2006 represents a significant shift in the right direction and is a vast improvement on the earlier, out-dated version.

There have been calls for greater public accountability in regard to the so-called wider interests, not only in the UK but in other jurisdictions. Stakeholder concerns are now a feature of many codes of corporate governance best practice around the world and are especially embedded in the successive King Reports on corporate governance in South Africa.

To summarize, in terms of governance and corporate ownership, a company as a person in its own right cannot be owned—and it is not owned by any one of its stakeholders including its shareholders.

3

The evolution of directors' duties

The common law about the duties of directors developed from the middle of the 19th century and established that they were the duties of good faith, loyalty, care, skill and diligence. In some countries these common law duties, developed over decades, have been written into corporate statutes, but reading it does not give it content and context. There is far more to written law than following the letter. The company once registered becomes a person in a country. It is not a living, breathing person like an individual but an artificial one who is absolutely incapacitated and inanimate. It has no heart, mind or soul. It is the directors who animate the company. In the formation of a company, the subscribers would have determined the business of the company and they would appoint its directors as the first shareholders of the company.

If an 18-year-old youth is injured in a motor car accident and a neurosurgeon advises his family that physically he is in great shape and will probably live well into his 90s but, as a result of the accident, he will have severe brain damage for the rest of his life, then the family gathers and appoints one of its members as the guardian of that person for the remainder of his life. Similarly, when an elderly parent develops dementia or Alzheimer's disease, the Court of Protection often appoints a son or daughter to act as representative for the parent, overseeing his or her finances, property, investments and also ensuring the parent's well-being and continuing care.

None of us would want members of our family or our friends to think of us as a guardian who is not acting loyally or in the unfortunate person's best interests. We would not contemplate filching any benefit for ourselves at the expense of an incapacitated child or a sick parent. We would, on an intellectually honest basis, apply ourselves in their best interests. This starts giving content to the duties of good faith and loyalty. We would take great care of their assets and we would voluntarily apply whatever skills we have in their interests in making decisions. We would be diligent in doing our homework in understanding their needs, interests and expectations and develop short-, medium- and long-term strategies for them.

These are exactly the duties of a director of an incapacitated company. The latter is more incapacitated than our unfortunate person with brain injuries or dementia. The company is more incapacitated because at least in the case of the young man the heart is still pumping and according to the great religions the soul is still in the body. Similarly, people with dementia are aware of their existence and have (if we choose to believe) a soul that is still intact. Our incapacitated artificial person has no heart, mind or soul of its own. The directors animate it, they become its heart, its mind, create its reputation and the trust and confidence that stakeholders have in it. We would also ensure that its operations were legitimate. We would act ethically and effectively by carrying out our duties with responsibility, accountability, fairness and transparency.

It is in the duty of care that directors are most likely to incur liability to a company because directors have to take risk for reward. Directors cannot be risk-averse out of self-concern. That would be a failure of their duty to the company. In taking risk and making decisions, no director is prescient in dealing with uncertain future events. From time to time all directors make the wrong business judgement call. Society, including the shareholders, accepts that this is so, provided that the directors acted with intellectual honesty at the time of making their decision and on an informed basis. This understanding has led to the development of the business judgment rule, a doctrine that exists in most commonlaw countries, which states that if directors are, objectively speaking, informed about a matter on which they are about to make a decision, they have no personal financial interest in the matter and it appears with the wisdom of hindsight that it was a rational business decision at that time in those circumstances, then even though the decision turns out to be the wrong business judgement call, and causes harm to the company, those directors would escape liability to the company.

In the duty to act carefully, directors must, in other words, not act negligently. The foundation of this duty is that directors have assumed the role of steering a company in certain directions that could cause harm to the company, and as such they are under a moral duty to perform that role carefully. There is no difference from doctors who are under a moral duty to carry out their professional duties carefully. To act carefully, directors need to have informed oversight of management's implementation of the decisions of the board, to make enquiry where information placed before them calls for enquiry and to ensure that their decisions appear to be rational, based on the facts and circumstances at the time.

In most jurisdictions the question of fulfilling the duty of care is tested objectively as to what a reasonable person with the equivalent knowledge of the director would have done in the particular circumstances. The general legal principle is that honest errors of judgement would usually not give rise to a cause of action but, as seen in the business judgment rule and in the requirements for carrying out the duty of care, a director has to ensure that they are informed decisions.

The enlightened shareholder approach requires directors to have regard to the interests of stakeholders other than shareholders on the basis that these interests represent a financially material issue for the company. Can this be sufficient where directors know or ought to know that the company's business model is impacting adversely on the environment when the company itself depends on the use of natural assets? Financial materiality is critically important but surely this *per se* is an inadequate basis for running a global multinational company whose effects and impacts are felt by society the world over? Some companies are as large in terms of financial wealth as the gross domestic product of small states. Companies can no longer be run on the basis of financial profitability alone when the repercussions of their actions and activities are so broadly felt.

In America, in some 30 states, and also globally, new generation of corporations are being registered, the so-called B Corporations. These are corporations beyond profit maximization for the benefit of shareholders to include society and the environment. They could not be sued as the Ford Motor Company was, being legally obliged to make sure that how the B Corporation makes its money has a positive impact on society and the environment.

If the inclusive approach to governance were adopted, as is discussed later, boards would have to make decisions in the best interests of the company, which is an international requirement, but in the decision-making process take account of sources of value creation, including the legitimate and reasonable needs, interests and expectations of all the stakeholders material to the business of the company. This is opposed to the exclusive approach to governance, which propagates the primacy of the shareholder.

It is argued that directors in the very changed world of the 21st century who continue to carry on business as usual are in fact failing in their duty of care to the incapacitated company that is so dependent on them, heart, mind and soul. It is known, or ought to be known, by the directors that the company is operating in a resource-deprived world, that natural assets are being used faster than nature is regenerating them and population growth continues. Consequently we have to learn to make more with less and carrying on business as usual is not an option.

In those circumstances, a board of directors who looks at only the (traditionally termed) financial aspects in its strategic thinking is failing to take account of the fact that the company operates in the triple context of the economy, society and the environment. In the 21st century we have to acknowledge that, first, many social and environmental issues are actually financial in nature and *not* non-financial, as previously termed. Further, it is critically important that where social and environmental factors are not obviously financial in their impact on a company, they may be substantial in terms of environmental degradation or societal welfare, and for these reasons alone they require attention from the directors. Companies such as Unilever have publically stated that they would no longer continue making quarterly reports and have linked their strategy to the impact that their products have on society. More recently, after the 17 Sustainability Development Goals were passed at the United Nations, many of the brands of Unilever have been linked to promoting those goals. John Montgomery, an American attorney, has written that what is required is for "directors to exercise the beginnings of a planetary consciousness" (Carl and Nguyen, 2012). Paul Polman, the Chief Executive of Unilever, urged stakeholders to hold companies accountable for their actions. He has publically stated that he does not believe it to be his fiduciary duty to put shareholders first and that Unilever's object and strategy is to improve people's lives, ensuring that the way they carry on business is done in a sustainable manner. He concluded that to do so would ultimately result, over the long term, in good shareholder returns. As early as 2009 he asked the following:

> Why would you invest in a company which is out of sync with the needs of society, that does not take its social compliance in its supply chain seriously, that does not think about the cost of externalities, or of its negative impacts on society?

The proof of the pudding is in the eating. The performance of Unilever since 2009 has in fact benefited shareholders. Not only that, but could any shareholder today have successfully launched a civil suit against Unilever to stop its long-term strategy of taking account of its sources of value creation, which include the legitimate and reasonable needs, interests and expectations of its material stakeholders?

It is submitted that directors who carry on business as usual, and believe that they do not have to change their business model even though it is having an adverse impact on society or the environment, in fact open themselves up to a claim for damages by the company when it suffers losses over the longer term, which is inevitable from such an approach in the changed world of the 21st century.

Global warming, climate change, the fact that we are experiencing the sixth period of mass extinction of life on earth, poverty in the developing world and disease are all realities of the 21st century that we cannot brush under the carpet or try to ignore. And 21st-century businesses, so huge in their scale and scope, are in a unique position to prevent chaos and the mass destruction of species and to abate global warming.

The shareholder-centric governance model has resulted in some inequitable outcomes from directors applying their duty of care in the best interests of the company but for the benefit of shareholders as a whole, while having regard to other stakeholders such as employees. The case of BHS Limited in the United Kingdom, founded in 1928, will become a locus classicus of the failure of a shareholder-centric approach, be it enlightened or otherwise. In summary, the majority shareholding of the group was purchased for £200 million and during the period of this shareholder being in ultimate control of the group, by means of a reduction of capital, the shareholder received dividends of £1.3 billion. A few years later the trading stores ran into liquidity problems and the shareholder sold its shares to a new shareholder for £1. Approximately a year later, the company was placed under administration and a few months later, into liquidation. At the time of liquidation (2016) 11,000 jobs were lost and the company's pension fund was short of some £500 million. There is no doubt that the dividends were paid at a time when it was lawful to do so in the sense of the company having readily realizable assets to pay its debts on due date or was in a cash flow position to do so. But if the board had applied its collective mind in making the decision of declaring that dividend to the sources of value creation, including the legitimate and reasonable needs, interests and expectations of the material stakeholders of the company (which must have included its employees), that dividend would probably not have been declared. It deprived the company of liquidity that might have enabled the company to have traded out of its difficulties. Certainly, the employees' pension fund would not have been short of some £500 million. This is a good illustration of how employees were unable to diversify their risk, but no doubt the major shareholder invested the dividends received and so diversified *its* risks.

Another poignant case of poor governance and lack of stake-holder responsibility, unfurling in the UK in 2016, is that of Sports Direct. Concerns about governance failure has attracted share-holder activism, with two major investment institutions, Legal & General Investment Management and Aberdeen Asset Management, criticizing Sports Direct heavily for its poor corporate governance. There have been calls for a trade-union-backed resolution to request an independent review of labour practices at the retail group as well as an independent review of the company's corporate governance more broadly. Staff have been paid effectively below the UK's mini-mum wage and there are serious concerns about the company's work practices. Britain's largest union is calling for significant change in employee contracts and treatment (Butler and Kollewe, 2016). Failure to treat all stakeholders fairly, in this case employees, is unacceptable for 21st-century companies committed to following corporate governance best practice codes.

It is apparent that for directors to discharge their duties in the best interests of the incapacitated company they should collectively consider the sources of value creation on a basis of parity. This is the inclusive approach to governance as opposed to the exclusive shareholder-centric model. Holistic governance is the only approach that will lead to enhanced societal welfare and proper stewardship of the natural world.

4

Exclusive and inclusive approaches to governance: moving towards holistic governance and accountability

The primacy of the shareholder in corporate governance has meant that directors would be seen to have a duty to act in the best interests of the general body of shareholders. Does that include all the different classes of shareholders? Which shareholders does it exclude? Does it mean all shareholders? Does it include a loan creditor who as collateral has cession of a shareholder's voting rights and its right to payment of a declared dividend? Those are all the shareholder's rights.

Shareholders are one group of a company's many stakeholders. A stakeholder is any party who affects or is affected by the company.[1] There are many major internal and external stakeholders, such as the directors, managers, employees, creditors, service providers, the community in which the company operates, and sometimes a regulator, depending on the nature of the business. As already pointed out, shareholders are in a better position than stakeholders such employees because a shareholder can diversify risk by investing in the equity of other companies. Employees cannot diversify their risk. In the broadest definitions, stakeholders can be interpreted as both human and non-human entities affected by a company's operations, extending stakeholder concerns to include the natural environment, flora and fauna, and future generations as yet unborn (discussed in Solomon, 2013).

The inclusive approach to governance demands that directors act in the best interests of the company but need to know the value creation sources, which would include the legitimate and reasonable needs, interests and expectations of the material stakeholders of the company. Likewise the company needs to inform these stakeholders what is expected of them. Clearly in the case of non-human stakeholders or future generations, this level of accountability is challenging, although communication with representatives of these stakeholders, such as wildlife non-governmental organizations (NGOs) in the case of the environment and species, is an effective proxy. Stakeholders are made up of parties who contract with the organization, for example, customers, employees or suppliers, and parties that have a non-contractual nexus with the organization, for example, civil society, local communities, NGOs and the environment. The state as legislator or regulator is also a stakeholder.

---

1   One of the earliest discussions of stakeholders and their role in corporate governance, which led to the development of 'stakeholder theory', was the work of Freeman (1984).

Stakeholder relationships have to be managed. A board needs to know who are the company's major stakeholder groupings and what are their legitimate and reasonable needs, interests and expectations of the company. Without having this information the board has an uninformed oversight over management's proposals on strategy. And management, if it did not know the needs, interests and expectations of the stakeholders, for example its customers, would be developing an uninformed strategy.

Academic work focusing on stakeholder engagement processes has shown that they can only succeed where the engagement is not dominated or "captured" by the company's management. This implies that stakeholder engagement should benefit both management and stakeholders equally and should be dialogic in nature. Historically, researchers found from observing stakeholder engagement meetings and forums that they tended to be dominated by management interests and suffered from capture by the more powerful parties in the room. Researchers suggest that for stakeholder engagement to work properly it needs to adopt the model of "ideal speech situation". Ideal speech means that all parties have equal ability to speak and be listened to and that no one person or group in the discussion and dialogue should control the "conversation".[2] Although developed from academic theory, the concept of ideal speech being applied to corporate stakeholder dialogue is extremely

---

2   The concept of the "ideal speech situation" arises from the work of the German critical philosopher, Jürgen Habermas, who describes his concept as follows: "[I]f all participants in dialogue have the same opportunity to... initiate communication and continue it through speaking and responding of asking questions and giving answers, then... equally distributing the opportunities to put forth interpretations, assertions, explanations, and justifications and to establish or refute their claims to validity—can be a way of creating a basis on which no prejudice or unexamined belief will remain exempt from thematization and critique in the long run" (Habermas, 2001, p. 98).

useful. Indeed, this framework was used to analyse the absence of effective stakeholder engagement in the takeover of Cadbury by Kraft, with the finding that there was little attempt made to engage with employees prior to the takeover or in the ensuing aftermath (See Barone *et al.*, 2013).

A company's relationships with stakeholders have become of such importance in the 21st century that many companies have appointed a new corporate "animal" called the corporate stakeholder relationship officer (CSRO). His or her job is to communicate with stakeholders on an ongoing basis, learn of their legitimate and reasonable needs, interests and expectations and feed this information to management. Management then develops strategy on a more informed basis. The CSRO also does a report to the board at each board meeting that has an agenda item "stakeholder relationships" on the "state of play" with stakeholders.

A CSRO must be capable of integrated thinking around all the resources or capitals being used as inputs by the company into its business model and the outcomes of the company's product or service. He or she should be an experienced executive who understands business value propositions and the interdependence between resources used, the business model, the product and stakeholder relationships. The CSRO must understand the triple context in which the company operates and be a good communicator and networker. Every board should agree on the purpose of the business of a company and the main value drivers of the business. The board should also agree on the character of the company as opposed to the culture of the company. The character of the company may be understood as those specific attributes associated with the company that arise from the perceptions of stakeholders of the company from its conduct as a corporate citizen.

The responsibilities of a CSRO involve focusing on interactive ongoing strategic communication between the company and its core stakeholders. By channelling communications from external stakeholders towards the organization and management, the CSRO can assist management to manage on a more informed basis. Stakeholder engagement and the role of the CSRO are also crucial to identifying the material social, environmental and economic issues relevant to a company, which must then be filtered into the integrated report. Benefits arising for the company from the CSRO's activities should include:

- Improved strategic decision-making

- Enhanced organisational reputation among stakeholders

- Identification of business opportunities and risks that could otherwise have been missed

- Continual assessment of the company's business model to ensure its sustainability and competitiveness

- Ensuring that the company's governing structure has identified the social, environmental, financial, human, manufactured and intellectual capital issues that impact on the business and ensuring they are embedded into corporate strategy

In addition to evident benefits to the company, an effective CSRO who elicits proper stakeholder engagement processes and stakeholder dialogue should engender important benefits for the stakeholder groups themselves.

It is essential that a CSRO's job description includes a practical application of what we have referred to as an ideal speech situation, in that all parties need to be given equal voice and equal ability to influence the debate. Outcomes from stakeholder engagement should be the "best" for all parties, independent of the views of the most powerful participant. An effective CSRO can enact genuine stakeholder inclusivity and dialogue. Stakeholder engagement represents a core mechanism of holistic governance and stakeholder responsibility.

The board should identify the major stakeholders of the business of the company and be informed and know their legitimate and reasonable needs, interests and expectations. In the decision-making process it takes account of the sources of value creation including those needs, interests and expectations but always makes a decision in the best interests of the company. This could result in one stakeholder being preferred above another but subsequently the reverse could happen. The critical issue is that the board at the start of the decision-making process gives parity to the different sources of value creation but makes a decision in the best interests of the company—not in the best interests of any one stakeholder.

As an illustration of how important the role of the CSRO may be, a listed mining company has just spent two years with its CSRO speaking to a community about the positive impact on that community when they start mining and extract the gold that their geologist has said is situated in that community. The benefits are that property values will increase, business needs will increase, an extra hotel will have to be built and so on. There is also an undertaking on how the land will be rehabilitated when the mining of gold is no longer feasible. Consequently, not a pebble has been turned for two years while this communication with stakeholders, particularly the community in which the mine will operate, has taken place. This sort of stakeholder dialogue is essential to the building of trust relationships with local communities who will undeniably be deeply affected by the company's activities. Further, in a world characterized by the immediacy of the internet and the prominence of social media, it is vital that stakeholder dialogue and negotiation precedes any activity that may have deleterious impacts, in order to protect and enhance corporate reputation and avoid reputational and ethical disasters. From a more theoretical perspective, this form of stakeholder engagement is far closer to the concept of ideal speech.

Compare this approach with the situation arising from the oil spill in the Mexican Gulf, the Deepwater Horizon case involving BP plc in 2010. The impact of this massive spill had on the communities around the Gulf of Mexico was, to put it mildly, horrendous. Fisheries were devastated as was the whole ecosystem in that vast area of sea and marine life. There was, it appears, no relationship, ongoing or otherwise, between the company and that important stakeholder, the local community that was so adversely affected by the spill. In the wake of the event BP has spent millions and millions of pounds clearing up the effects of the spill and has demonstrated substantial responsibility to local populations and the natural environment. If only this level of care to environmental and ecological risk had sparked alarm bells about the oil platform before the event all the distress and social/ecological impact could have been averted.

There is no doubt as we progress through the 21st century that stakeholder relationships and stakeholder dialogue are intensely important and relevant to corporate strategy, corporate communications and should precede corporate actions.

Part II

The dawning of a new era of corporate reporting

In the second part of this book, there is first an exploration of the roots of accounting, and especially bookkeeping, from a historical perspective. Then we discuss sustainability reporting, its evolution and the establishment of the International Integrated Reporting Council (IIRC). Third, there is a discussion of how the corporate world is shifting in the 21st century, with the growing need for inclusive governance and capitalism, leading to the necessary development of integrated reporting and integrated thinking. This discussion culminates in a consideration of the "new order of corporate reporting", focusing on the integrated report providing an ideal vehicle for companies to disclose information relating to the six capitals, sustainable development goals (SDGs), the Aichi targets and "extinction accounting".

5

From financial reporting to corporate reporting

Luca Pacioli was a merchant of Venice who lived in the creative age of masters such as Leonardo da Vinci. He observed how the merchants recorded their transactions. This drove him to write a thesis in 1494 that became the foundation of double-entry book-keeping as we have known it for the last 500 years. Merchants were able now to identify and measure financial capital for the first time. The financial statements of companies based on the double-entry system resulted in the reporting of historical financial matters from which the user could learn little in order to make an informed assessment about the ability of a company to maintain value creation in a sustainable manner. In 1945 Unilever published its annual report with separate notes about the balance sheet and the profit and loss statement. It also had a schedule of capital expenditure and a diagram of the company's organizational structure. Accounting researchers have described this as laudable information provided by the company! (This breakthrough report is explored in Camfferman and Zeff, 2003.)

Towards the end of the 20th century an analysis of companies listed on great stock exchanges showed that the book value of companies as reflected in their financial statements according to financial reporting standards made up only 30% of the market capitalization of these companies. The question arose, what assets were the investors placing a value on? The answer was clearly that they were the so-called intangible assets, specifically:

- How the company devises its long-term strategy to maintain value creation

- The company's reputation in the market place

- What happens in the company's supply chain

- Whether the company has a supply chain code of conduct and whether it is being monitored?

- The relationships between the company and its major stakeholders

- How the company makes its money, in other words does it have a positive impact on society and the environment?

- Where the company has a positive impact on society and the environment, how are these positive impacts being enhanced?

- What negative impacts the company has on society and the environment and how these are being eradicated or ameliorated

- The quality of the company's governance

- The quality of the company's risk management

- Whether the company's internal controls are adequate and effective

All this became pertinent because the world had changed. It had changed dramatically in the 1960s when the third industrial revolution started with the computer age. By the beginning of the 21st century, climate change was becoming a critical issue. Ecological overshoot was a reality, namely the use of natural assets faster than nature was regenerating them. Through social media there was radical transparency. There was greater expectation from stakeholders than ever before, with a new energetic activism from stakeholders, particularly civil society. There had been a population explosion, with the United Nations indicating that by 2045 there would probably be another 2 billion people on Planet Earth (UN, Department of Economic and Social Affairs, 2015).

We have now entered the fourth industrial revolution, only 30 to 40 years since the third. The fourth industrial revolution includes artificial intelligence, robotics, nano-technology, 3D printing, analytics and the internet of things. In the context of all the above, some great companies concluded that they could not carry on business as usual. They had to learn to make more with less.

Further, the duty of accountability was called into question. It was clear that financial statements alone, although critical, were not sufficient to tell the user about, for example, the intangible assets. There were innovations in corporate reporting such as enhanced business reporting, balanced score cards, and sustainability reporting developed with the establishment of the Global Reporting Initiative (GRI) in Boston (later moving to Amsterdam). Each of these was trying to communicate the value creation by the company involved.

In short, in the 21st century we moved beyond financial reporting. The International Federation of Accountants (IFAC) agreed that financial reporting, although critical, was not sufficient. The GRI, the gold standard of sustainability reporting, agreed that sustainability reporting, although critical, clearly without the numbers was not sufficient. And the two, each reporting in a silo, did not reflect the reality of what was happening on the ground.

In every company resources are used and there is an ongoing relationship between the company and its stakeholders. These are interconnected and interrelated on a daily basis. The sources of value creation are not in separate buildings. There is a symphony of resources used and relationships with stakeholders.

Historically, there have been various attempts to initiate a more stakeholder-inclusive approach to accounting and reporting, but they have had little success in changing mind-sets. One of the earliest attempts to integrate "intangible" assets and broader corporate responsibilities in accounting was the publication of *The Corporate Report* (ASSC, 1975). It is probably fair to say that this report was ahead of its time and for that reason was unable to take hold within the business community. *The Corporate Report* recommended additional statements to be included in the annual report, aimed at wider stakeholder groups than just shareholders, including a statement of value added, an employment report, a statement of money exchanges with government, a statement of transactions and foreign currency, a statement of future prospects and a statement of corporate objectives. Similarly, the (abandoned) Operating and Financial Review in the 1990s represented a serious attempt to make social and environmental reporting mandatory within the annual report, as we saw earlier.

Despite various unsuccessful attempts at operationalizing forms of social and environmental accounting within accounting practice, there has been a long and lively debate within the international academic accounting community. Most notably, the work of Professor Rob Gray and many other colleagues from the UK, Australia and elsewhere has led to the formation of an extremely significant body of academic work developing theories of social and environmental reporting, investigating the philosophical, cultural and moral bases of such reporting and making recommendations for practice. This has culminated in the creation and maintenance of a global network of accounting academics fully engaged in researching accounting for the environment and social accounting, under the auspices of the Centre for Social and Environmental Accounting Research (CSEAR), which now operates chapters worldwide. It has also led to the establishment of leading journals devoted to researching social and environment, sustainability and social responsibility reporting such as *Accounting, Auditing & Accountability Journal* and *Accounting, Organizations and Society*. These publications are by no means concerned solely with developing academic theory and idealism but often present practical, research-led solutions to current issues which a clear focus on pragmatism and praxis.

The main academic research focus has been on stand-alone social and environmental or, more recently, sustainability/corporate social responsibility (CSR) reports. The dawning of integrated reporting has led us in a different direction with integration of those earlier separate reports into the heart of the annual reporting vehicle produced by listed companies. Ironically, the success of integrated reporting could be seen as the end of the stand-alone sustainability report.

In 2006 the Prince of Wales started the Accounting for Sustainability (A4S) project, contending that the impacts on society and the environment of how a company makes its money should be connected to financial reporting. A4S started promoting connected reporting.

Meanwhile in South Africa, the King Committee on Corporate Governance had in 1994 promoted the inclusive governance approach, and King II published in 2002 recommended sustainability reporting as a listing requirement. King III (2009) made integrated reporting based on integrated thinking a listing requirement for all companies with a primary listing on the Johannesburg Stock Exchange.

Integrated thinking recognizes that there are at least six inputs into the business of every company, namely financial, human, natural, manufactured, social and relational and intellectual capitals. The activities of a company create its business model or how the company makes its money. This embraces the quality of governance, enterprise risk management, the strategy for the business and the oversight by the board of management's implementation of the board's decisions. The company then produces its product. The product goes out into society and the product in turn has an outcome in society. Integrated thinking is an integration of the process of inputs to outcomes involving the resources or capitals used by the company including the ongoing relationships with its stakeholders. In the Framework of the IIRC, issued in December 2013, integrated thinking is defined as

> The active consideration by an organization of the relationships between its various operating and functional units and the capitals that the organization uses or affects. Integrated thinking leads to integrated decision-making and actions that consider the creation of value over the short, medium and long term (IIRC, 2013, p. 4).

Inputs are defined as "the capitals (resources and relationships) that the organization draws upon for its business activities". Outcomes are defined as "the internal and external consequences (positive and negative) for the capitals as a result of an organization's business activities and outputs". Outputs are defined as an organization's "products and services and any by-products and waste".

It will be seen that integrated reporting embraces the inclusive approach to governance.

The IIRC issued a document about inspiring innovation and a new role for the accountancy profession. I adapt that document to demonstrate the move away from reporting only the financial statements.

As we saw in the first part of this book, in the 20th century we witnessed the development of capital markets. Stock markets were created to raise finance and resulted in the dispersion of shareholding. With this development the necessity for corporate reporting emerged. Financial crises, corporate scandals, the growth of international accounting standards and the globalization of capital markets had led to the introduction of new market regulators, standards boards, legislation and regulation in accounting and corporate reporting. By the late 20th century, a new rigid design of regulation and enforcement had been imposed across most of the world's major capital markets.

The effect of taking the design of the accounting ecosystem away from the accountancy profession and placing it in the hands of regulators has been to lose the flexibility and market alignment that has been such a key element of having an accounting ecosystem that is consistently fit for purpose. The role of the accounting profession as the designers of the accounting ecosystem brought a degree of innovation ensuring the system itself remained fit for today and tomorrow. This capacity for innovation has been lost and, instead, the design implementation and oversight of the system is in different hands. There are layers of complexity and isolated methodologies, metrics and disclosures set apart from strategy or the connection to other resources and the business model. Many of the new requirements have been imposed in response to crisis or scandal, the effect of which has been to build a compliance regime, many layers of boilerplate disclosure and, now, voluminous reporting.

Even within the constraints imposed by regulation, accountants have found the capacity for innovation. The profession is well represented in the accounting standard-setting arena and the late 20th century gave birth to one of the most innovative developments in the history of accounting: a new accounting language, International Financial Reporting Standards (IFRS) and US Globally Accepted Accounting Principles (GAAP).

It is impossible to make the case for a change to the corporate reporting system without consideration of the changed business landscape within which corporate reporting reform fits. This includes a significant shift towards greater transparency, which is transforming the relationship between business and its principal stakeholders.

These developments are taking place at the same time that doubts are emerging about the role of finance in society—whether finance has become too dominant a factor in the decision-making of governments and capital markets. The question that flows from these concerns is whether financial development has limits. It is certainly the view of the International Monetary Fund (IMF) and the Bank of International Settlements that the dominance of finance and the speed with which financial developments take place within economies can both exacerbate short-termism and contribute to financial instability. This issue has come into sharp focus recently as income inequality is seen by many policymakers to be a brake on economic development.

The economic community has played a key role in both conceptualizing and contextualizing this changed business landscape. Other reporting innovations include value reporting, enhanced business reporting, balanced scorecards, triple bottom line and sustainability reporting—each of which has brought out an emphasis on identifying and communicating value creation in a broader sense. Each has brought a development to the ecosystem of corporate reporting. Individual companies such as Nestlé (through the adoption of Michael Porter and Mark Kramer's concept of Shared

Value [Porter and Kramer, 2011]) and Puma (Environmental Profit and Loss Account [EP&L]) have become associated with specific initiatives that have been adopted internally. *One Report: Integrated Reporting for a Sustainable Strategy*, published by Professor Bob Eccles and Mike Krzus (2010), crystallized the thinking of many.

The world's financial system has faced multiple crises, destroying value and potential for a whole generation. It is a world in which population growth and climate change are putting pressure on the availability of natural resources—resources that are critical to business success. Leading figures such as Christine Lagarde, Managing Director of the IMF, and Mark Carney, Chairman of the G20's Financial Stability Board, are calling for the adoption of a new inclusive system of capitalism.

The new movements, including the work of the Coalition for Inclusive Capitalism and Focusing Capital on the Long Term as well as Integrated Reporting, have completely changed corporate thinking and reporting.

While Pacioli's double-entry system was purely financial, integrated reporting has spearheaded an inclusive, multi-capital approach to reflect value creation in a knowledge-based, natural-resource-constrained global economy. Integrated reporting matches double-entry book-keeping for its global applicability and its resonance to the needs of today's business and society. Integrated reporting has forged new connections in the 21st century between business and society—a new language of impacts and outcomes is becoming part of the norm. It is bridging the divide between financial, social and natural capitals.

This new development in the field of corporate reporting opens up an opportunity for the accountancy profession to reclaim its historic role in charge of the design and system of accounting and corporate reporting, to embed the incentives and measurement within business and across markets. The role of the accountancy profession remains of strategic importance to the whole economy. The accountant's capacity for innovation has ensured the enduring relevance of the profession. In an era of radical change, that capacity for innovation is needed today more than ever before.

The question arises, how do accountants reclaim their role as the designer of the system of accounting and corporate reporting? The answer lies in the education of students studying accountancy, so that the accountant is no longer focused on financial capital but appreciates that the company is a critical part of society and how it makes its money has an impact on the economy, society and the environment. Depending on the nature of those impacts the company's market value will be determined because it will affect the valuation placed on its reputation, the trust and confidence that stakeholders have in the company and the very legitimacy of its operations. Many corporate finance textbooks and financial reporting books have still not incorporated climate change finance, for example, or issues of sustainability reporting, despite entering their tenth or sometimes even later edition.

The following sections discuss the explosion on requirements of environmental, social and governance (ESG) reporting, the changed thinking on value creation for corporations, the shifts in the corporate world and the concept of integrated reporting—a concept whose time has come.

6

Sustainability reporting and the establishment of the IIRC

By 1997 it was realized that the additives in a balance sheet according to financial reporting standards that had by then been created did not equal the market capitalization of companies. In fact the market cap exceeded those additives by between 70% and 80%. This included the intangible assets of strategy, reputation, supply chain conduct, stakeholder relationships, controls, risk management, the positive and negative impacts of how the company makes its money and the quality of its governance. Nowhere is it better illustrated than in an analysis of the S&P 500 that is set out in Figure 6.1.

FIGURE 6.1   Components of market value

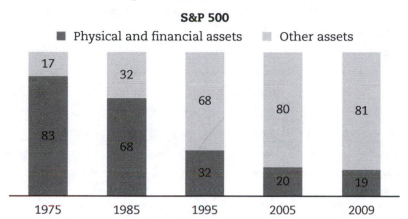

Components of market value

S&P 500

Source: CIMA

This led to thought leaders Allen White and Bob Massie to start drafting guidelines on how companies could report on these so-called intangible assets. They formed the Global Reporting Initiative (GRI) in Boston. In 2002 there was the World Summit in Johannesburg and Allen White and I met, the result of which was that the King Committee on Corporate Governance in South Africa recommended in 2002 that sustainability reporting should be a listing requirement on the Johannesburg Stock Exchange. As Chairman of the United Nations Committee on Governance and Oversight, I learnt that the work being done by the UN Environmental Programme and the UN Community for Trade and Development clearly indicated that the exclusive approach to governance was something that could not be maintained.

For economic, tax and other reasons the GRI moved from Boston to Amsterdam and I became its chairman. Sustainability reporting has gained huge momentum. In America the Sustainability

Accounting Standards Board has been founded. The GRI is also developing standards for ESG reporting. The European Union has issued a directive for large companies to prepare ESG reports. Several stock exchanges have made it a listing requirement, and the filings with the Securities and Exchanges Commission in America contain more sustainability issues.

The Prince of Wales had started Accounting for Sustainability (A4S) in 2006. That trust was doing work on connected reporting, connecting the impacts of a company's activities on society and the environment with its financials. A meeting between the leaders of A4S and me as chairman of the GRI resulted in the prince graciously agreeing to host a meeting of the who's who of corporate reporting at St James's Palace at the beginning of 2010. By that time, the King Committee had recommended integrated thinking and reporting as a listing requirement in what became known as King III.

The global chairmen of the Big Four auditing firms, the World Bank, the International Organization for Securities Commissions (IOSCO), the executive director of the World Wide Fund for Nature (WWF), the chairman of the Financial Accounting Standards Board of America, the chairman of the International Accounting Standards Board, A4S, GRI, investors, regulators and major corporations were invited.

All invitees came to the meeting, which was chaired by Sir Michael Peat who was then the treasurer to the Royal Household and was also intimately involved with A4S. Paul Druckman, the past president of the Institute of Chartered Accountants of England and Wales was the chairman of A4S. Sir Michael asked me to address the meeting on integrated thinking and "doing" an integrated report. Arising out of that meeting the International Integrated Reporting Council was formed consisting of the bodies who were present and inviting other international bodies onto the Council. I was charged with the duty of appointing the chief executive and

I appointed Paul Druckman. Paul and I, the IIRC board and executive together with the input from many professionals and executives from around the world created the Integrated Reporting Framework of December 2013. Today there are some 70 IIRC members, which include the great accountancy bodies around the world, regulators, investors and other institutions. The membership of the IIRC can be found on its website at theiirc.org.

An integrated report requires the collective mind of the board to spend more time understanding the financial statements prepared according to financial reporting standards and the sustainability data collected by most companies today in addition to a sustainability report according to standards. The matters material to the business of the company are placed in clear, concise and understandable language integrating the financial and sustainability information. This will enable the user to make an informed assessment of whether the business of the company will maintain value creation in a sustainable manner.

The financial statements in IFRS or US GAAP speak have become incomprehensible to the average user. Hence the requirement in the Framework for the report to be in clear, concise and understandable language. An integrated report is defined in the IIRC Framework as "A concise communication about how an organization's strategy, governance, performance and prospects, in the context of its external environment, lead to the creation of value in the short, medium and long term."

What is important is to accept that to discharge the duty of a board to be accountable, its report has to be understandable. The organization must have all the financial and sustainability information available online enabling users to drill down to obtain the detail they require.

ESG factors have become critical in the changed world of the 21st century. No board can discharge its duty of accountability without having regard for ESG factors affecting a company and reporting on those so that the reader can make an informed assessment about how the company is making its money.

In addition to the European Union's directive that their major companies have to do ESG reports, there are the sustainability filings with the US Securities and Exchange Commission, and Australia has developed the Operating Financial Review, which is a narrative and analysis to supplement the financial report, to assist "in understanding the operations, financial position, business strategy and prospects of an entity". The Australian Securities and Investment Commission goes on to say in its Regulation 247.42 that the disclosure may include how the entity makes its money, how it generates income or capital growth for shareholders and how otherwise it achieves its objectives.

In the UK the strategic report has become a requirement of the Financial Reporting Council. The strategic report is a step away from an integrated report as understood in the Framework of the IIRC.

Social and relationship capital has become critical. Andrew Haldane, in his speech "The great divide" (2016) has pointed to the divide between financial and social capital. In the speech Haldane records that social capital is inextricably linked to trust and distinguishes between personalized trust and generalized trust:

> Personalised trust refers to mutual co-operation built up through repeated personal interactions—for example like visits to the doctor or hairdresser. By contrast, generalised trust is attached to an identifiable, but anonymous, group—for example trust in the rule of law, or government or Father Christmas.

He then goes on to point out that banks were local and the service was customized and personalized. The mystique of its operations created a generalized trust among the public. In the modern era the business model of banking has changed. Local branches went into retreat, the local branch manager began to disappear, service became centralized, personalized trust was lost and banking came to rely for its legitimacy on an ever greater degree of generalized trust. When the financial crisis hit, "it dealt a hammerblow to generalised trust in banking too. Anonymity gave way to ignominy, blissful ignorance to blistering resentfulness" (Haldane, 2016).

This gives impetus to the philosophy that each company has its own society, made up, inter alia, of its internal stakeholders, employees, managers and so on and the general society in which it operates. A company cannot carry on business contrary to the expectations and mores of the general society in which it operates. Seen through the lens of personalized and generalized societies, it is clear that society, as a whole, is the licensor of a company. This claim has driven a change to the Milton Friedman philosophy and a mind-set change.

It is also a major driver of the explosion in the requirement of ESG reporting around the world. The other major driver is an understanding that Planet Earth is at a tipping point. It is a resource-deprived planet with demands being made on its resources beyond its capacity if business is carried on as usual.

A map drawn by researchers at Harvard University on global corporate social responsibility disclosure requirements shows by country the recent requirements by governments and stock exchanges of ESG disclosure.

7

Shifts in the corporate world

The IIRC, working together with many of its council members and associates, has concluded that there are three major shifts in the corporate world.

First, there is the shift from silo reporting to integrated reporting. This is a recognition that financial reporting on its own is critical but not sufficient. The same applies to sustainability reporting. For a company to have both reports but in silos does not reflect the reality of the company's operations and functions, which are interconnected and interrelated.

This led to the famous meeting at St James's Palace, the formation of the IIRC and the publication of the Framework with guidelines on how to think on an integrated basis and to do an integrated report. The Framework sets out general principles and the content elements of an integrated report.

The traction for integrated reporting around the world has been nothing short of phenomenal. This is because it is a concept whose time had come once great international bodies on financial and sustainability reporting such as IFAC and the GRI had recognized that financial or sustainability reports in silos were critical but not sufficient. The board needs to spend more time applying its mind to the mass of data being collected today and extract that which is material to the business of the company and put it in clear, concise and understandable language in an integrated report.

That such reporting is required is evidenced from the statement by Larry Fink, CEO of BlackRock, in an open letter which he wrote to the CEOs of the European Union and the United States of America. In his letter Mr Fink urges CEOs to resist "the powerful forces of short-termism afflicting corporate behavior", asks for CEOs to "lay out for shareholders each year a strategic framework for long-term value creation" and says that "CEOs should explicitly affirm that their boards have reviewed those plans" (Turner, 2016).

The next day the Chartered Financial Analysts of the United States issued a statement. Referring to this letter, Sandra Peters (Head, Global Financial Reporting Policy) and James Allen (Head, Capital Markets Policy—Americas Region) of the CFA Institute, wrote a letter to the *Financial Times* in which they noted that

> Efforts by the International Integrated Reporting Council to develop a framework for reporting value creation seem very much in line with what Mr. Fink is suggesting. We have encouraged accounting standard-setters and policymakers globally to think more broadly about reporting on strategic objectives as well as about environmental, social and governance (ESG) factors (Peters and Allen, 2016).

The second major shift is from a financial capital market system to an inclusive capital market system. In 2013 Lynn de Rothschild hosted a meeting at the Lord Mayor of the City of London's residence, Mansion House, in which the speakers included Christine Lagarde from the IMF, Bill Clinton, former US president, and Paul

Polman, the chief executive of Unilever. The result of that meeting was the formation of the Coalition for Inclusive Capitalism.

Inclusive capitalism is a move away from the focus on financial capital, looking at how a company makes its money and the impact which it has on the three critical aspects of the economy, society and the environment. Aid is given by the developed world to the developing world. This is not a sustainable model, but when the great multinational enterprises, some operating in 140 countries, operate on a basis of embedding into their strategy the material sustainability issues concerning the business of the company, then in the developing country the outcome should be a more positive impact on society and the environment. In consequence, the quality of life in that developing country should improve. The Coalition for Inclusive Capitalism has accepted that the way to achieve an inclusive capital market system is for organizations, both public and private, to adopt integrated thinking and do an integrated report.

The third major shift is from a short-term capital market to a sustainable capital market. The plague of short-term profit, or, as Hillary Clinton has called it, the tyranny of quarterly reporting, has resulted in a focus of profit-making for the benefit of shareholders, notwithstanding that it might be at a cost to society and/or the environment.

This plague of short-term profit was a major contributor to the global financial crisis. Directors have been steering public and private organizations down the street of last opportunity in a resource-deprived world, exacerbated by population growth with its consequential increased demand for product. As we saw earlier, short-termism has been acknowledged as a problem linked to an agency approach that is clearly outdated and not fit for purpose in this century.

The board of a company, in order to discharge its duty of care, has to take account of the positive and negative affects of how the company makes its money on the three critical aspects. The company will create value in a sustainable manner by enhancing the positive affects and eradicating or ameliorating the negative affects. If in making its money it is doing so with adverse affects on society or the environment, then it could be destroying value or transforming one of the resources or capitals used by the company.

Sustainable capitalism is a shift in corporate behaviour so that the company maintains value creation but in a sustainable manner.

A company having as its business the brewing of beer would have a long-term strategy to reduce the use of water, replenish, reuse and recycle water. Water is the scarcest natural commodity on Planet Earth and without such a long-term strategy, the board would be failing in its duty of care to the company. It is an example of the positive affects in a resource -deprived world of an inclusive governance approach. The board of the company operating the brewery would apply its collective mind in the best interests of the company, taking account of the sources of value creation, which would include the legitimate and reasonable needs, interests and expectations of its material stakeholders.

8

Integrated thinking and the integrated report

Integrated thinking involves the board as a collective understanding, knowing and then planning how the company will make its money. In other words it must determine the company's business model, embracing its governance, enterprise risk management, strategy and internal controls. It will also consider how the company will maintain value creation in the longer term in a sustainable manner. In order to do this the board has to determine the inputs into its business activities, the outputs from those business activities and the effects that its outputs have on the resources used by the company, more particularly the effect it has on society and the environment—the social and natural capitals.

Every company is dependent on the resources it uses and the ongoing relationships with its stakeholders. A mind-set change is needed at the board and senior management level to accept that there is this interconnection and interrelationship between the use of resources by the company and the company's relationships with its stakeholders. There is, as it were, a symphony of sources of value creation that includes the relationships with material stakeholders on an ongoing basis, 24/7.

No company operates on a basis of financial capital in one building, human capital in another, intellectual capital in another city, for example. All these things are interrelated and interconnected.

Once management is aware of the legitimate and reasonable needs, interests and expectations of all its material stakeholders, it can strategize on a more informed basis. It needs to be aware of what is occurring in it supply chain, as it is now well known that what happens in a supply chain can destroy value, particularly the value of a company's intangible assets. For example, if it is found that in the supply chain products supplied to the company were made by child labour, this would adversely impact on the market capitalization of the company.

In thinking on an integrated basis, the board needs to identify the sustainability issues material to the business of the company, as water is to the beverage manufacturer, and embed those sustainability issues into its long-term strategy. In this way it will be discharging its duty of care to the company.

In the IIRC's Framework of December 2013 (p. 34) integrated reporting, integrated thinking and the integrated report are defined as follows:

> *Integrated Reporting (<IR>):* A process founded on integrated thinking that results in a periodic integrated report by an organization about value creation over time and related communications regarding aspects of value creation.
>
> *Integrated thinking:* The active consideration by an organization of the relationships between its various operating and functional units and the capitals that the organization uses or affects. Integrated thinking leads to integrated decision-making and actions that consider the creation of value over the short, medium and long term.

Integrated report: A concise communication about how an organization's strategy, governance, performance and prospects, in the context of its external environment, lead to the creation of value in the short, medium and long term.

In a talk given by Paul Druckman, the Chief Executive of the IIRC, to the United Nations Economic and Social Council, he described three stages of integrated thinking.

He started with Einstein's definition of insanity of "doing something over and over again and expecting a different result". If one believes that the corporation need only deal with financial capital issues and fulfil its duty of accountability merely by providing financial statements according to financial reporting standards and duly audited according to International Standards of Auditing, then one is effectively doing, over and over again, the same thing and expecting a different result in the changed world of the 21st century. One cannot from that, for example, determine value creation. In fact the business model chosen by the company could be destroying value.

The second stage is an acknowledgment that there is a problem by merely complying with the law and doing the financial statements according to the accepted standards. A new solution is required, but it cannot be based on the old thinking. Again, Einstein said : "We cannot solve our problems with the same thinking we used when we created them".

Consequently, a strategy that only considers the financial aspects of a company and does not concern itself with how the company makes its money and how it impacts on the various resources used by the company has not embedded sustainability issues into its strategy. And not to do so would amount to a failure of the board's duty of care to the company.

The third stage is where all six capitals as outlined in the IIRC's Framework, namely financial, manufactured, human, natural, intellectual, social and natural capitals, are considered together with the ongoing relationships with the company's material stakeholders. It is accepted that there is an interconnection between the resources used and the relationships with material stakeholders. The board concerns itself with how the company make its money and how that business model impacts on the outcomes on those capitals.

It certainly starts to inform decision-making, and once the board spends more time understanding the mass of data being collected by companies, and taking the matters material to the business of the company and putting them in clear, concise and understandable language in the integrated report, knowledge does not get lost in information.

Value creation could result in increases, decreases or transformation of the capitals being used and the outcomes are internal and external. A company's success depends on its internal financial return but in the changed world of the 21st century it has to also depend on the external return on society and the environment.

The Association for Chartered Certified Accountants (ACCA) has said the following about integrated reporting:

> Over the past few decades, sustainability issues have slowly become mainstream, and there is a shift from the creation of share value to the generation of shared value. Through shared value creation, a company links its operations to generating long-term value both for its business and for society as a whole and defines its success in terms of internal financial returns and external social and economic results. Ultimately, creating shared value acknowledges both the work that corporations need to do to reduce negative impacts on society as well as, and more fundamentally, how they can be part of progress on global challenges, such as climate change and the enforcement of human rights. Following this shift, there is a new trend of corporate reporting: the integration of financial and nonfinancial concerns into one accounting tool, known as IR.

Black Sun, an independent research house, in interviewing several companies that were pilot programmers in adopting integrated thinking and doing an integrated report, summarized the information received from these companies on the benefits they got from implementing integrated reporting as follows:

1. **Connecting departments.** One of the most mentioned benefits of integrated reporting is the opportunity it provides to connect teams from across an organization, breaking down silos and leading to more integrated thinking.

2. **Improved internal processes leading to a better understanding of the business.** Changes to systems driven by integrated reporting requirements are providing greater visibility across business activities and helping to improve understanding of how organizations create value in the broadest sense.

3. **Increased focus and awareness of senior management.** A shift to integrated reporting is increasing the interest and engagement of senior management in issues around the long-term sustainability of the business, which is helping them to gain a more holistic understanding of their organization.

4. **Better articulation of the strategy and business model.** Better understanding of organizational activities is enabling companies to establish a holistic business model and helping to streamline communications.

5. **Creating value for stakeholders.** Organizations are starting to identify ways to measure the value to stakeholders of managing and reporting on sustainability issues.

The integrated report shows how a company creates value over time. This process is influenced by the company's external environment, its stakeholders and the resources it uses. This will result in increases, decreases or transformations of the resources triggered by the company's operations.

There are two interrelated aspects of value. Value is created for the company itself with a financial return that enables the company to pay its creditors and a dividend to shareholders, short-, medium- and long-term cash flow needs permitting. The ability of a company to create value for itself is linked to the value it creates for its stakeholders.

IFAC, the Chartered Institute of Management Accountants and PwC have drawn up lists of the possible inputs into a business, a business's activities, its outputs and possible outcomes (IFAC *et al.*, 2013):

Inputs

The six capitals, which may take the form of:

- Funding model

- Infrastructure

- People

- Intellectual property

- Raw materials

- Ecosystem services

- Relationships

Activities

- Research and development

- Planning

- Design

- Production/conversion
- Product differentiation
- Market segmentation
- Distribution
- Service provision
- Quality control
- Operational improvement
- Relationship management
- After-sales service

Outputs

- Products
- Services
- Waste
- Other by-products

Outcomes

- Customer satisfaction
- Profit/loss
- Shareholder return
- Asset consumption
- Contribution to local economy through taxes
- Job creation
- Employee development and engagement
- Improved standard of living

- Environmental impact

- Licence to operate

These three organizations make it clear that the above lists are not intended to be exclusive. Depending on the business there may well be other inputs, activities, outputs or outcomes.

In recognition of the need to take account of how the company makes its money and the effect it has on the two critical aspects of society and the environment, a circular economy is now being developed. Business models are being reorganized along biological rather than industrial lines. Organizations are starting to deliver customer value without waste and with ability to recycle the products they produce after use. Interface, a carpet manufacturing company, has developed carpet tiles for commercial premises that are not made from fossil-fuel-based raw materials. It is a polymeric material floor covering with 99.7% less waste and can be reused and recycled. The company saves 80% greenhouse gas emissions and 87% water use. It has almost no landfill issues. This is a business that is maintaining value creation in a sustainable manner.

In our resource-deprived and overpopulated world integrated reporting really is a concept that could lead to financial stability and sustainability.

9

The new order of corporate reporting

A phenomenon of the last 20 years or so is the emergence and veritable explosion of responsible investment activity.[1] From the availability of dedicated portfolios for "ethical investors" in the last century we have seen an emergence of responsible investment as an effective and powerful mechanism of corporate governance and accountability. Investor engagement and dialogue were identified by the late Sir Adrian Cadbury, in what became known as the Cadbury Report, as an important tool for driving improvements in corporate governance (see Corporate Governance Committee, 1992). The growing practice of institutional investor engagement with companies on ESG issues is calling companies to account for their impact on society and the natural environment and forcing them to take issues seriously, on the basis that they are financial and definitely not "non-financial".

1   A review of the development and current state of responsible investment around the world is contained in Hebb *et al*. 2015.

Although, as we saw earlier, shareholders are not really "owners" they still have a tremendous potential to affect corporate behaviour. They have voting rights, and boards for this reason, rather than ownership, take notice. Rather than selling their shares, large institutional investors can alter corporate behaviour and strategy through engagement and dialogue and active shareholding.

The Principles for Responsible Investment (PRI), an initiative in partnership with the United Nations Environmental Programme Finance Initiative (UNEPFI) and the United Nations Global Compact, were developed by an international group of institutional investors reflecting the increase in relevance to asset owners and managers of ESG issues. The process was convened by the UN Secretary-General. Some $60 trillion of asset owners have agreed to embrace the Principles, Ban Ki-moon, the United Nations Secretary-General said in April 2006,

> By incorporating environmental, social and governance criteria in their investment decision making analysis processes, the signatories to the Principles are directly influencing companies to improve performance in these areas. This, in turn, is contributing to our efforts to promote good corporate citizenship and to build a more stable, sustainable and inclusive global economy.

These great asset owners acknowledge that they have a duty to act in the best long-term interests of their ultimate beneficiaries. In this regard, they believe that ESG issues can affect the performance of investment portfolios. They have committed to the PRI. First, they undertake that they will incorporate ESG issues into their investment analysis and decision-making processes; they have started advocating ESG training for investment professionals and have encouraged academic and other research in this area. Second, these great asset owners undertake to be active owners and incorporate ESG issues into their ownership policies and practices, and they have started engaging with companies on ESG issues and seek to file shareholder resolutions consistent with long-term ESG considerations. Third, they undertake to seek appropriate disclosure on ESG issues by the entities in which they invest. They are asking for standardized reporting on ESG issues and that ESG issues be integrated within annual financial reports. Fourth, they undertake to promote acceptance and implementation of the PRI within the investment industry and they have started supporting tools for ESG integration.

Because of the shareholder-centric model of governance, one of the frequently asked questions is, what are the implications in applying the PRI for a director's fiduciary duties, particularly a director's duty of care to a company? The UNEPFI and the Global Compact have answered this question on the basis that it is undeniable that ESG issues can affect investment and performance, and that the appropriate consideration of these issues is part of delivering superior risk-adjusted returns and is therefore firmly within the bounds of the investor's fiduciary duties in this context. Concomitantly they must also be within the bounds of a director's duty to act in the best interests of the company.

The PRI, originally endorsed by the United Nations, has resulted in some countries developing their own stewardship codes for responsible investment, such as in the United Kingdom and South Africa. These stewardship codes drive integrating ESG issues into investment decisions. The Stewardship Code[2] published in the UK in 2009 arose from the aftermath of the banking crisis as a recommendation from the Walker Review (2009) into the causes of the crisis and how further similar events could be avoided. The South African Code for Responsible Investment in South Africa (CRISA)

2   Financial Reporting Council. https://www.frc.org.uk/Our-Work/Codes-Standards/Corporate-governance/UK-Stewardship-Code.aspx.

was published by the Institute of Directors in Southern Africa (2011) and members of the South African investment community have identified the Code as a driver of integrated reporting, stating that CRISA was developed partly to assist pension fund trustees in establishing their fund's ESG mandate.[3]

Consequently, it will be seen that for the raising of capital, directors in fulfilling their duties to a company need to ensure that how the company makes its money is impacting positively on the environment and society. From a governance point of view it must not be a mindless quantitative exercise but quality governance.

Quality governance requires that the board as a collective applies its mind on an intellectually honest basis to the issue at hand and takes into account the sources of value creation, which include the ongoing relationship between the company and its stakeholders. The board needs to be focused on value creation in the long term rather than in short-term profit-making. To do otherwise would lead to "a tragedy of the horizons" as Mark Carney has described it.

The plague of short-term profit and the "tyranny of quarterly reporting" as stated by former secretary of state Hillary Clinton has to move to an inclusive capital model so that the activities of the company have positive impacts on the economy, society and the environment.

There is now a directive for ESG reporting in the European Union, and in this regard Richard Howitt MEP, who sponsored the non-financial reporting directive and is now CEO of the IIRC, endorsed integrated reporting as the right step for companies implementing the directive to enhance transparency and support sustainable development. During the event, Erik Nooteboom (head of

---

3   These findings arose from research interviews conducted in South Africa and published in Atkins and Maroun 2014.

accounting and financial reporting for the European Commission) said: "Personally, I think integrated reporting is a necessity, it is unavoidable and it will come."

The six capitals model results in the board giving parity to the six capitals in ensuring that how the company makes its money has positive impacts on the three critical aspects or will be ameliorating and eradicating negative impacts.

The Natural Capital Protocol represents a standardized framework to identify, measure and value direct and indirect impacts (positive and negative) and dependencies on natural capital where natural capital has been defined as the stock of renewable and non-renewable natural resources (e.g. plants, animals, air, water, soils, minerals) that combine to yield a flow of benefits to people (see Atkinson and Pearce, 1995; Jansson *et al.*, 1994; Natural Capital Coalition, 2016). The Protocol provides a basis for businesses to assess their impacts and any material risks arising to the business. In essence, the approach encapsulated in the Protocol involves integrated thinking, integrating concerns about natural capital, nature, wildlife, biodiversity, greenhouse gas emissions and climate change into a company's business model and business strategy. This approach is entirely consistent with the work of the IIRC and integrated reporting provides the ideal means of disclosing information relating to a company's involvement in natural capital.

Another critically important development in the path towards a new world order and the emergence of reporting and accounting that are fit for purpose in the 21st century is the creation of the Sustainable Development Goals of the UN, developed in conjunction with the private sector. The 17 SDGs require organizations to ensure sustainable development and to put an end to hunger and poverty in all its forms. The final document for the SDGs, which was agreed in Addis Ababa, stated: "We will promote sustainable corporate practices including integrating environmental, social and governance factors into company reporting" (UN 2015) This is a shift towards an inclusive multi-capitals approach that delivers a more complete picture of value creation. When companies think about value creation in the long term, they are driven to think about future risks flowing from matters such as climate change and resource scarcity. More so is this the case with the Paris Agreement on climate change,[4] the SDGs and the UNPRI.

It is clear from the discussion throughout this book that if we are to protect the planet for future generations, ensure the safety of the human race and protect biodiversity then the attainment of the SDGs is essential. Further, it seems that integrated reporting represents the ideal vehicle for reporting on the achievement (or otherwise) of the SDGs. The 17 SDGs may be easily clustered according to economic, social and environmental factors and then reported within the integrated reporting framework. Furthermore, it seems a natural process for a corporation's integrated thinking to incorporate SDGs into this process. By way of illustration, we can cluster the goals according to the tenets of integrated reporting as follows, although arguably the clustering could be approached differently. Goal 7, for example, could be seen to fall under economic as well as social factors.

Mapping SDGs onto economic factors disclosed in integrated reports
Goal 8. Promote sustained, inclusive and sustainable economic growth, full and productive employment and decent work for all
Goal 9. Build resilient infrastructure, promote inclusive and sustainable industrialization and foster innovation
Goal 12. Ensure sustainable consumption and production patterns

4   UN Framework Convention on Climate Change. Retrieved from http://unfccc.int/paris_agreement/items/9485.php.

Mapping SDGs onto social factors disclosed in integrated reports

Goal 1. End poverty in all its forms everywhere

Goal 2. End hunger, achieve food security and improved nutrition and promote sustainable agriculture

Goal 3. Ensure healthy lives and promote well-being for all at all ages

Goal 4. Ensure inclusive and equitable quality education and promote lifelong learning opportunities for all

Goal 5. Achieve gender equality and empower all women and girls

Goal 6. Ensure availability and sustainable management of water and sanitation for all

Goal 7 Ensure access to affordable, reliable, sustainable and modern energy for all

Goal 10. Reduce inequality within and among countries

Goal 11. Make cities and human settlements inclusive, safe, resilient and sustainable

Goal 16. Promote peaceful and inclusive societies for sustainable development, provide access to justice for all and build effective, accountable and inclusive institutions at all levels

Goal 17. Strengthen the means of implementation and revitalize the Global Partnership for Sustainable Development

Mapping SDGs onto environmental factors disclosed in integrated reporting

Goal 13. Take urgent action to combat climate change and its impacts

Goal 14. Conserve and sustainably use the oceans, seas and marine resources for sustainable development

Goal 15. Protect, restore and promote sustainable use of terrestrial ecosystems, sustainably manage forests, combat desertification, and halt and reverse land degradation and halt biodiversity loss

In relation to environmental elements of integrated reporting, an alarming fact is that we are currently experiencing the sixth period of mass extinction of flora and fauna on planet earth. Many people do not realize the severity and speed at which species are being driven into extinction by human, industrial activity. Preventing further extinctions is a primary aim of the Convention on Biological Diversity's Aichi Biodiversity Targets[5] and the SDGs. Indeed SDGs 14 and 15 aim to conserve and sustainably use the marine environment and, "protect, restore and promote sustainable use of terrestrial ecosystems, sustainably manage forests, combat desertification, and halt and reverse land degradation and halt biodiversity loss". Further, SDG 15 states that by 2020 there should be protection and prevention of extinction of threatened species. The 12th Aichi target states that by 2020 the extinction of known threatened species will have been prevented and their conservation status, particularly of those most in decline, has been improved and sustained.

A *State of Nature Report* was launched in the UK in September 2016 (see Hayhow *et al.*, 2016.). The researchers found that over half (56%) of UK species studied have declined since 1970. Further, of almost 8,000 species assessed in the UK, more than a tenth are under threat of extinction. The report suggests that the UK is not on course to meet the SDGs on biodiversity and that far more work needs to be done to prevent extinction.

Biodiversity is a core element of natural capital. Companies have relatively recently started reporting information on biodiversity and efforts they are making to protect and enhance biodiversity in the areas where they operate and beyond. Companies especially in high environmental impact sectors such as mining, oil and gas, and tourism are providing the most significant quantity of biodiversity information. However, researchers have concluded that on the

5   www.cbd.int/sp/targets.

whole, although substantial funds are being dedicated to biodiversity action plans and strategies to preserve biodiversity, the approaches tend to focus on risk management (reputation, for example) and an "anthropocentric" approach, meaning basically the reporting revolves around species that are the most "useful" to the human race through the ecosystem services they provide (see, for example, Jones and Solomon, 2013; Atkins *et al.*, 2014). This means that species that are less cuddly or useful are to a great extent ignored. An integrated approach to the ecosystem and biodiversity has to acknowledge that all species in the planet's ecosystem are linked and that, despite science, we really have little idea what the impact of losing one species, even the tiniest insect, may have on the ecosystem as a whole.

Of most concern, to us at least as members of the human race, is the stark fact that if the ecosystem collapses due to extinction after extinction, then ultimately human life will also be under threat of extinction. We have only to consider the impact of losing one species, the bee, to see how this could be the case. Almost 15% of bee species across Europe are under threat of extinction. There are massive annual losses of commercial and wild bee populations worldwide due to a wide array of (human-led) factors. Put simply, no bees, no pollination, no crops, no food, no humans.[6]

Recognition of the urgency regarding the state of biodiversity and the current and growing extinction crisis has now led to a form of "extinction accounting". There are two GRI Principles devoted to species at risk of extinction according to the International Union for Conservation of Nature (IUCN) categorization. Section G4-EN14 of the GRI Principles requires companies to provide disclosures relating to species, by level of extinction risk, categorized

---

6   For greater detail on the financial and accounting implications of bee decline see Atkins and Atkins, 2016.

as critically endangered, endangered, vulnerable, near threatened, of least concern, by the IUCN Red List. The guide to the GRI Principles suggests that disclosing this information should encourage companies to alter their behaviour in respect of these species. However, it is our contention that merely following this group principle will leave a "fossil record" of species. We need to do far more than that. We need a form of accounting that will aid the fight against extinction rather than record it for posterity.

A framework for extinction accounting has been developed that goes far further than the GRI Principles.[7] This framework includes the stages shown in Table 9.1. The intention of the framework is that it involves companies doing far more than merely reporting on threatened species but effectively forces them into action, reflection and further action. In this way the framework intends to be transformative, or in the terms of the academic accounting community, "emancipatory".[8] Emancipatory extinction accounting represents a mechanism of ecological governance that can, and hopefully will, prevent the extinction of species worldwide. *Accounting can save the planet*. A forthcoming book assesses the extent of extinction accounting by companies around the world and also explores the potential for responsible investors and NGOs to drive corporate change in relation to threatened species.[9]

---

7   The extinction accounting framework was first presented on 24 September 2015 at the Dundee University Staff Seminar series and is contained in Atkins *et al.*, 2015.

8   The concept of "emancipatory accounting" was developed in a seminal book, *Accounting and Emancipation: Some Critical Interventions* (Gallhofer and Haslam, 2003). This has been further researched and refined in Gallhofer *et al.*, 2015.

9   Atkins, J. and Atkins, B. (eds.) (forthcoming) *Around the World in 80 Species: Exploring the Business of Extinction* (Sheffield, UK: Greenleaf Publishing).

TABLE 9.1   **Extinction accounting: reporting stages for extinction prevention**

Stage	Action
Stage 1 (Stage 1 is equivalent to the existing GRI principles)	Record a list of plant and animal species, identified as endangered by the IUCN Red List, whose habitats are affected by the company's activities Report where, geographically, the company's activities pose a threat to endangered plant and animal species, as identified by the IUCN Red List Report potential risks/impacts on these specific species arising from the company's operations
Stage 2	Report actions/initiatives taken by the company to avoid harm to, and to prevent extinction of, endangered plant and animal species
Stage 3	Report partnerships/engagement between wildlife/ nature/conservation organizations and the company which aim to address corporate impacts on endangered species and report the outcome/impact of engagement/partnerships on endangered species
Stage 4	Report assessment and reflection on outcome/ impact of engagement/partnerships and decisions taken about necessary changes to policy/initiatives going forward
Stage 5	Report regular assessments (audit) of species populations in areas affected by corporate operations
Stage 6	Report assessment of whether or not corporate initiatives/actions are assisting in prevention of species extinction
Stage 7	Report strategy for the future development and improvement of actions/ initiatives: an iterative process

Source: Atkins *et al.* 2015

As with the reporting of SDGs, integrated reporting provides a natural vehicle for extinction accounting. Indeed, only integrated reporting could bring this type of critical ecological form of reporting and disclosure into the heart of corporate reporting. The devil is in the detail. It is this level of detail and the need to incorporate detailed information about species and efforts to protect them and reverse the extinction trend that are crucial to saving the natural world, of which we are one integrated element. Again, integrated reporting that integrates SDGs, extinction accounting, bees and bee decline and any factor that has an impact on society, the environment or the economy can, and in our view, will, save Planet Earth.

The conclusion from all the above is that we have a new order in regard to companies. A board that, in the context of the PRI and the SDGs, ignores these principles and goals will result in the company having great difficulty in raising capital and will probably result in the company not being seen as a good corporate citizen. This would have a negative impact on the market capitalization of the company. It also results in another conclusion, namely that the shareholder-primacy thinking that applied in Dodge v. Ford Motor Company and the enlightened shareholder approach are against the new order of things.

Central to agreements on the SDGs and on climate change was consideration of the role of the private sector and its reporting practices in helping to achieve the desired outcomes. The ACCA and the Climate Disclosure Standards Board (CDSB) have said that there is a growing realization that the assessment of corporate performance relies on information about financial, social, environmental and governance issues, "There is a widely recognised premise that economic, social and environmental systems are interdependent and that their continuance relies on limiting the use, trading and exchange of environmental assets, goods and services in line with planetary boundaries (Guthrie, 2016, p. 13)."

The megatrends drive recognition that companies need to go beyond enhanced profit-making for shareholders and recognize that what benefits people and the planet also benefits enterprise.

> Enterprises are being called on to create shared value and inclusive growth, which works on the basis that inclusion of stakeholder interests and corporate planning and activity can lead to competitive advantage, a stronger licence to operate,

enhanced reputation and more sustainable practices (Guthrie, 2016, p. 15).

In dealing with the new order that I have tried to describe above, ACCA and CDSB say:

> The new order of corporate reporting demands both past results relating to an organisation's use and consumption of and effect on various "capitals" as well as evidence on how its strategy and long-term goals are designed to contribute to sustainable outcomes (Guthrie, 2016, p. 15).

In a comparison of the old and new orders of corporate reporting, they list the points set out in Table 9.2.

TABLE 9.2   The old and new orders of corporate reporting

The old order of corporate reporting	The new order of corporate reporting
Long and cluttered	Concise and material
Boilerplate language	Effective communication
Backward looking and short term	Forward looking and longer term
Complex	Simple and easily navigable
General purpose	Sensitive to audience needs
Focused on financial results for shareholders	Focused on value creation for the organization and its stakeholders
Rule bound, narrow disclosure	Transparent and responsive to individual circumstances
Reflects stewardship of financial capital	Reflects stewardship of all forms of capital on which the organization is dependent and that it affects
Locked in, static	Technology enabled

Source: Guthrie, 2016, Table 1.1.

We have attempted to bring together global and international initiatives in this part of the book to demonstrate the way in which integrated reporting can assist companies in reporting on issues of critical significance to the survival of the planet including the United Nation's SDGs, the Natural Capital Protocol, the Aichi Targets and an emergent form of extinction accounting (see Figure 9.1).

FIGURE 9.1   How Integrated reporting can save the planet: integrated reporting as a vehicle for reporting on Sustainable Development Goals, the Natural Capital Protocol, the Global Reporting Initiative, the Aichi Targets and extinction accounting

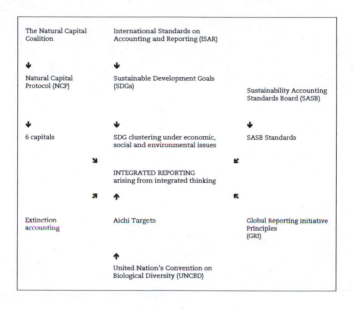

Part III

Value creation and the chief value officer

This part of the book explores value creation and provides a framework incorporating mechanisms that are crucial to ensuring value is created. Consolidating holistic governance, stakeholder inclusivity, integrated reporting and the creation of the **chief value officer (CVO) role** provides the most effective and responsible means of value creation. The following sections address in turn: value creation; the success of integrated reporting and the ways in which integrated reporting leads to value creation; the role of the CVO; and last, but not least, the need to transform accounting education and the training of accountants (as well as the training of financiers, analysts and investors).

10

Value creation

As we have seen, from the late 1990s it was known that up to 80% of market value was made up of so-called intangible assets. Institutional investors, in order to discharge their duty of care to their beneficiaries, have to assess the long-term strategy of a company, its reputation in the society in which it operates, how it is monitoring its supply chain, its relationships with its stakeholders, the quality of its governance and whether its business activities are creating positive or negative impacts on the three critical aspects of the economy, society and the environment.

Book value means the value of the business of a company according to its financial statements. It is a difference between a company's total assets and total liabilities. This also equates to shareholder value because, after paying off total liabilities, if there is a positive difference, the last stakeholder in the queue, namely the shareholder, would receive that value.

Market value is the value as indicated by the trading in the shares of the company listed on a stock exchange. The number of shares issued multiplied by the price established by market forces will determine the price of the share. The number of shares issued times that price is the market value of the company. When the book value is greater than the market value it means that stakeholders have lost confidence that the company can maintain value creation and in a sustainable manner. Brutally put, it means that stakeholders do not accept the company's ability to continue to perform positively as a going concern. Where the market value is greater than the book value this reflects a belief and confidence that the company will create value in a sustainable manner, long term. Through a financial lens it means that earnings will be increasing. Where book value equals market value it is an indication that stakeholders have no belief that there is going to be any increase in value and probably means that the company has not communicated a long-term strategy that indicates that the company has positive earnings generation or value creation in the longer term.

Book value is determined by the additives in a balance sheet according to financial reporting standards and total liabilities. This is historical financial information without knowing the company's business model and the impact of its outputs on the six capitals. This historical information on only one aspect of the company's activities will not assist an investor in making an informed decision whether to invest in the equity of that company or not. The other financial measurement on value has been the present value of discounted future cash flows, given a specific rate of return. The discount rate must be appropriate in order to properly value future cash flows. It will be seen that these two financial measurements do not take account of the critical capitals other than financial. In applying the six capitals models of the IIRC the board gives parity to all six capitals.

Integrated reporting helps a company to create value and tell its story. Indeed, the evolution of the "corporate narrative" is vitally important to a company's image and reputation, which all contribute to value. It helps create value because directors are able to better understand and connect the drivers of long-term value, which enables better strategy formulation. The user of an integrated report can understand in clear, concise and understandable language how value has been created more effectively, both internally and externally, and connect the drivers of long-term value.

The following quotations (taken from Tomorrow's Company, 2014) are indicative of this creation of value.

> <IR> gives an opportunity to clearly communicate your strategic message—what is our business model? how do we create value? what is our relationship with a broad view of stakeholders? and critically why is our business model sustainable in the long term?… and we think this is a question that a number of users are challenging corporates to answer (Russell Picot, Chief Accounting Officer, HSBC)

> The distinction between reporting on value creation and creating value is an important one. Better reporting leads to better understanding which should lead to better value creation (Alan Stewart, Chief Finance Officer, M&S).

> Economic value is a forward and not a backward looking concept and rarely are reporting frameworks prepared to grasp this nettle. Management should use the opportunity through the <IR> Framework to provide its view of the future (qualitative and quantitative) and then be prepared to be held accountable in the future as to the outturn against previous projections of value creation (Ken Lever, Chief Executive, Xchanging)

> Integrated Reporting facilitates a holistic approach to management; combining financial data with environmental, social, governance and other issues to inform corporate strategy which is why it is relevant to C-level executives (David Blood, senior partner, and managing partner at Generation Investment Management LLP).

> For decades, investor decision-making has been governed by information in financial statements. In today's world, how effectively a company addresses sustainability issues can impact

its financial position and future prospects. The concept and practice of Integrated Reporting is advancing because companies and investors increasingly acknowledge that an integrated understanding of performance—one that connects drivers of long-term value—s needed in order to make informed decisions Dr Jean Rogers, CEO & founder, SASB.

In July 2014 the American Institute of Certified Public Accountants (AICPA) and Chartered Institute of Management Accountants (CIMA) surveyed 393 CFOs, CEOs and COOs from across the world; 94% of these executives said it was important for them to be able to explain how their businesses created value; 92% of them felt that bringing financial and non-financial information together helped them to better explain how their businesses created value over time.

Charles Nichols, the group controller at Unilever, has said:

> We live in a volatile world where businesses such as Unilever face issues that need long-term solutions. It is therefore natural that organisations and business leaders are thinking about how they encourage a long-term perspective internally and how this should shape the way they tell their story externally. Back in 2010, we launched the Unilever Sustainable Living Plan, aimed at building a more sustainable business model for Unilever. This was the catalyst to start thinking differently about the way we do business. This meant adopting a more integrated approach to measuring progress within our business and how we report externally to our various stakeholders against our long-term vision—to double the size of the business whilst reducing our environmental footprint and increasing our positive societal impact. IR is a very powerful framework for thinking about our business model and the way we create value. There are enough highly publicised examples of corporate failures where it became clear that even boards did not know how their particular organisation was creating value and the risks that they were taking. Driving sustainable long-term performance starts with a deep understanding of your business model and a clear articulation of what success looks like.

From this flows strategic alignment, the right metrics – financial and non-financial – and an appreciation of business risks. All these are prerequisites for a sustainable, high performing business. The IR Framework encourages the kind of integrated thinking that we need to drive performance internally and report our progress externally (Tomorrow's Company, 2014).

Frank Curtiss, the Head of Corporate Governance at RPMI Railpen Investments has said in regard to understanding how a company creates value:

> I have been a supporter of Integrated Reporting since its inception both as an investor and through my involvement in the International Corporate Governance Network.
>
> Financial accounting has evolved over time, but it does not tell the whole story. Neither is it forward looking enough. Current financial accounting does not take into account long-term macroeconomic factors which are vital in making long-term investment decisions such as human and natural capital. These are important aspects of a company's business model and strategy. Most investors understand this and only a few focus just on the numbers. The regulatory trend is towards increasing reporting requirements and investors need to be careful not to add to this trend. Better reporting is not about "throwing in the kitchen sink" as this leads to unmanageable data and clutter. It is about relevancy and appropriateness of information. IR provides a framework for all the important factors to be better understood and communicated. It offers the possibility for harmonised, standardised data and comparability. At its best it helps a company explain how it creates value and so enables investors to make better investment decisions. Although reporting is used by many different audiences, I think it is important to remember that investor primacy and a clear narrative in the voice of management are key elements in risk reporting. High quality reporting increases investor confidence, not just in terms of the risks being discussed, but also in the overall quality of management. Senior management have to get involved in the process of IR, it encourages a flow of better management information and helps join up different

information sources across functional silos. In this way IR promotes cultural change and behaviour, fostering integrated thinking and a shared understanding of how the company creates value (Tomorrow's Company, 2014).

In Figure 10.1 it will be seen that natural, social, human and intellectual capital just cannot be ignored. To strategize taking into account only financial and manufactured capital would obviously not be giving parity to the sources of wealth creation, which would include taking account of the legitimate and reasonable needs, interests and expectations of stakeholders material to the business of the company.

FIGURE 10.1   The six capitals

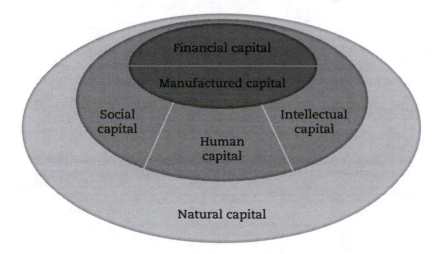

In the final draft leading to the Framework, the IIRC set out a graphic to show an organization's value creation process (see Figure 10.2).

FIGURE 10.2 An organization's value creation process

Source: IFAC et al. 2013, p. 1.

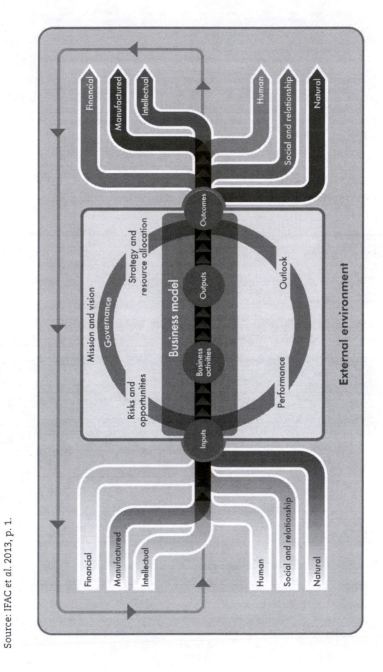

It will be seen that the inputs involve the six capitals. In making decisions the collective mind of the board is applied to these capitals on a basis of parity. But decisions have to be made in the best interests of the company. It follows that from time to time one stakeholder benefits more than another, but it is justified by being in the best interests of the company. The requirement of fairness in dealing with the company's stakeholders drives the board to understand the legitimate and reasonable needs, interests and expectations of stakeholders. It should also drive the board to discuss at each board meeting the inputs into the business model, the model itself and the outcomes of the company's outputs. That is why there should be an agenda item at each board meeting of inputs to outcomes so that the board has to deal with the value creation process at each meeting.

Value is no longer looked at through a financial lens. It is rather looked at through a long-term sustainability lens. How does the company make its money and what are the positive and negative impacts on the triple aspects from its business model? Enhancing the positive impacts and eradicating or ameliorating the negative impacts is part of the value creation process. It is also necessary for the board to identify the critical sustainability issues material to the business of the company and embed those sustainability issues into its strategy, for the short, medium and long term.

The Coca-Cola Company, several years ago, appreciating that water was a finite natural asset on Planet Earth devised its long-term strategy of reusing, replenishing, reducing the use of and recycling water. A few years ago the board of Coca-Cola had to deal with the allegation of sugar causing obesity in children. This allegation arose from civil society in America and Mexico. The board was compelled to address the outcomes of the company's output, namely Coca-Cola. Their marketing strategy was to record that they believed that an active lifestyle leads to better living. They undertook that they would not advertise to children under the age of 12, they would have nutritional labelling on all their cans and bottles, they would make their various products with as low a calorie count as possible and at all their bottling plants around the world they would encourage exercise for children under the age of 12. It will be seen that, strategically, the board of Coca-Cola was now dealing with inputs to outcomes. It had in the past focused on its output, namely the product, in building Coca-Cola as the most valuable brand in the world (until Apple became the most valuable brand).

Value can no longer be looked at just through a financial lens. It has to be looked at through the prism of the inputs into a company, its activities and the outcomes of those activities and outputs. It is viewed through a sustainable lens giving parity to the sources of value creation, which include the legitimate and reasonable needs, interests and expectations of the company's material stakeholders.

Goedhart *et al.* (2015) make some pertinent remarks on value creation:

> Creating shareholder value is not the same as maximizing short-term profits—and companies that confuse the two often put both shareholder value and stakeholder interests at risk. Indeed, a system focused on creating shareholder value from business isn't the problem; short-termism is...

> we do believe that companies are better able to deliver long-term value to shareholders when they consider stakeholder concerns ...

> the evidence makes it clear that companies with a long strategic horizon create more value. The banks that had the insight and courage to forgo short-term profits during the real-estate bubble earned much better returns for shareholders over the longer term. Oil and gas companies known for investing in safety outperform those that haven't ...

we agree that for most companies anywhere in the world, pursuing the creation of long-term shareholder value requires satisfying other stakeholders as well.

We would go even further. We believe that companies dedicated to value creation are healthier and more robust—and that investing for sustainable growth also builds stronger economies, higher living standards, and more opportunities for individuals. Our research shows, for example, that many corporate-social-responsibility initiatives also create shareholder value, and managers should seek out such opportunities. For example, IBM's free web-based resources on business management not only help to build small and midsize enterprises but also improve IBM's reputation and relationships in new markets and develop relationships with potential customers. In another case, Novo Nordisk's "Triple Bottom Line" philosophy of social responsibility, environmental soundness, and economic viability has led to programs to improve diabetes care in China. According to the company, its programs have burnished its brand, added to its market share, and increased sales—at the same time as improving physician education and patient outcomes.

Applying a shareholder-centric model, be it enlightened or one of primacy, will result in a focus on the internal outcomes of financial capital. This is only part of the value creation process.

11

The benefits of integrated reporting

PwC in its 19th Annual Global CEO Survey (May 2016) reports on how CEOs think about incorporating ESG factors into the strategy of a company. It is clear from the survey that the 1,400 CEOs interviewed in 83 different countries are seriously addressing stakeholders' needs. The survey also shows that CEOs today know that the business of the company that they are leading is interconnected with society, the environment, and a regulator if it is pertinent to the business of the company.

The megatrends have created a new road on corporate behaviour and reporting. The megatrends were enough to result in 193 UN member states working together with the private sector to develop the SDGs to create "dignity for all" and "leaving no-one behind". Paraphrasing the 17 SDGs, it's about alleviating poverty, hunger and inequality and having regard to the megatrends such as climate change and a resource-deprived world. It is clear that strategy premised on a financial basis alone will not result in a business model that deals with the changed world of the 21st century.

In the PwC CEO survey the following questions were asked: "Who's influencing your strategy?" and "What impact do the following wider stakeholder groups have on your organisation's strategy?" The answers are revealing: 90% of them said customers and clients influence their strategy, 69% government and regulators, 67% industry competitors and peers, 51% employees, 48% supply chain partners, 41% providers of capital including investors, 30% general public, local communities, media, and 9% NGOs. Approximately 80% of the 1,400 CEOs are making changes to minimize their companies' social and environmental impacts.

It cannot be contended that any one of those CEOs is not acting in the best interests of the company by not focusing solely on the interests of the company's shareholders. It is clear that there is now a general acceptance that the company is a critical part of society. It is the chosen medium through which business is conducted and through which members of society are employed and value is created for the economy of that society. These CEOs have accepted that they have to redefine business success. They have accepted that business success cannot be measured by a simple set of financial statements. The survey shows that 86% of these CEOs are responding to stakeholders' needs, interests and expectations in developing strategy and 76% of them agree that business success in the 21st century will be redefined by more than financial profit.

In April 2016 the International Federation of Accountants issued a statement as follows:

> The importance of sustainability and corporate responsibility continue to gain recognition; indeed, organizations that embrace sustainability can enhance their reputation with stakeholders and their value. The intersection of business and sustainability has three key dimensions: the economic viability, social wellbeing and environmental responsibility. Accountants work in this area to help embed sustainability factors into

an organisation's strategy and decision-making processes to achieve sustainable value creation.

Integrated thinking helps a board to understand the extent to which the business of the company depends on and how it impacts on social and natural capital. It is known that businesses rely on nature and society for survival. A report from CIMA, EY, IFAC and the Natural Capital Coalition (CIMA *et al.* 2014) includes recommendations on how CFOs should raise natural capital as a strategic issue and make the business case for it.

Natural capital is the foundation for all the other forms of capital, including financial, but natural assets are being depleted faster than nature is regenerating them. It is estimated that by 2030 we will need the natural capital of two planets to maintain growth if we do not change corporate behaviour in both the public and private sectors. We do not have two planets. We have to learn to make more with less. This means carrying on business as unusual as many great companies are doing, for example Unilever, Toyota and Interface.

Lean Production, pioneered by Toyota, has enabled many organizations to deliver high-quality products at a low cost and now business models are being created along biological rather than industrial lines. Biological or circular systems of production is a natural progression. Waste occurs at two points, in the creation of the product and eventually in its disposal after it has been used. Some businesses are now creating their outputs in a manner that reduces emissions and are having virtually zero waste to landfill. One example, already mentioned in Section 8, is Interface, the floor covering business, which has reduced waste by 99% and water use by 87%. Its greenhouse gas emissions are down by 80%. It will be seen that it is driving a circular economy by recycling the used product, which clearly delivers a social benefit and has a positive impact on the environment.

In 2016 IFAC published *Creating Value with Integrated Thinking: the Role of Professional Accountants* to

> highlight the important role accountants play in integrated thinking. Integrated thinking and reporting provides a means and an additional incentive for CFOs, and their finance teams, to focus on the information and the decisions that matter to the organisation and its potential success... the principles and concepts of integrated thinking and reporting are a natural progression on their journey.

Black Sun, in its two surveys on the benefits of adopting integrated thinking and doing an integrated report, has shown that 71% of the participants experienced strategic benefits, the most important being a change in conversations between the board and management; 79% reported improvements in management information and decision-making; and 96% experienced a positive impact from connecting departments and broadening perspectives.

As early as 2011, KPMG, in their survey of corporate responsibility reporting, recognized the beginnings of a shift towards integrated reporting, concluding that,

> While our research has included a number of very basic forms of integrated reporting, we believe the ultimate 'end state' would combine financial and CR [corporate responsibility] reporting as part of a comprehensive approach to reflect the company's full business performance for its key value drivers against the company strategy in an integrated way (KPMG, 2011).

The reality is that integrated reporting has resulted in financial and non-financial performance no longer being separated and an organization accepting that one affects the other and vice versa. The organization's strategy is shared by all functions and divisions and decision-making is being carried out with a longer-term view on value creation.

But it is not only the private sector organizations that will have appreciated this. Public sector organizations are also starting to strategize on a basis of embedding the sustainability issues relevant to an organization into its strategy and including in strategy the outcomes of its product or service. Bertrand Badre of the World Business Group said:

> Public sector entities are some of the largest, if not the largest, reporting entities in the world, so the transparency of their financial information is of importance to us all. Integrated reporting would enable governments and their stakeholders to gain a better understanding of resources available and help them to manage these more effectively.

The Global Commission on Economy and Climate has recommended that businesses should adopt and implement the IR Framework. The Japanese Ministry of Economy, Trade and Industry has endorsed integrated reporting as a means of communicating the long-term value creation proposition of companies and is encouraging Japanese companies to become best practice leaders in integrated reporting. The International Corporate Governance Network has as one of its principles that the board should provide an integrated report (ICGN, 2014). The ESG directive in the EU, the Strategy Reports in the UK and the Operating Financial Review in Australia are just one step from doing an integrated report.

Integrated reporting is tacitly supported in the open letter written by Laurence Fink, the chief executive of BlackRock to the chief executives of companies in the EU and the US, in which he urges CEOs to resist "the powerful forces of short-termism afflicting corporate behavior" and asks them to "lay out for shareholders each year a strategic framework for long-term value creation" and says that "CEOs should explicitly affirm that their boards have reviewed those plans" (Turner, 2016).

This was followed by an express reference to IR by the Chartered Financial Analysts (CFA) of America in response the next day to Larry Fink's letter, through Sandra Peters and James Allen, who wrote in the *Financial Times*:

> Efforts by the International Integrated Reporting Council to develop a framework for reporting value creation seem very much in line with what Mr Fink is suggesting. We have encouraged accounting standard-setters and policymakers globally to think more broadly about reporting on strategic objectives as well as about environmental, social and governance (ESG) factors (Peters and Allen, 2016).

The Prime Minister of Sri Lanka said in 2015: "Learning and adopting Integrated Reporting will definitely benefit the corporate sector and make their reports more meaningful to investors and stakeholders. This will make our country more attractive for foreign direct investment and local private investment" (quoted in Global Sustain, 2015).

Integrated thinking and "doing" an integrated report were concepts whose time had come, once it was accepted that financial reporting alone was critical but not sufficient, and likewise for sustainability reporting. Further, once intangible assets took on greater value than the tangible assets recorded as additives in a balance sheet according to financial reporting standards, there had to be a change in corporate reporting. Add to that the Principles of Responsible Investment and the megatrends in the changed world of the 21st century and it is clear that carrying on business as usual or reporting as usual are no longer options. Companies cannot solve 21st-century problems with the same mind-set that their boards had when they created these problems. Boards cannot solve 21st-century challenges with 20th-century decision-making or reporting standards.

The intergovernmental working group of experts on International Standards of Accounting and Reporting (ISAR) on the integration of ESG information into corporate reporting are cooperating with UNCTAD to try to develop indicators on achieving the SDGs. There is a consultative group supporting this work. The two organizations held a conference at the United Nations Headquarters in Nairobi to discuss how the private sector could contribute to the attainment of the SDGs in the way they reported the incorporation of the SDGs into their business models. Although the question posed to the panel was on sustainability reporting, it was generally agreed that the SDGs fell into three clusters: the economy, society and the environment. Sustainability reporting deals with social and environmental issues while the Financial Accounting Standards Board (FASB) and the International Accounting Standards Board (IASB) deal with standards for financial reporting. The reporting of the balance sheet, profit and loss statements and sustainability report in silos do not reflect how an organization is operating as the sources of value creation, including the ongoing relationship between the organization and its stakeholders are interrelated and interconnected. It was argued at this panel discussion that integrated reporting was the form that could incorporate how an organization was striving to achieve the SDGs.

Unilever has accepted that sustainability is a critical part of the long-term value creation of its business. In regard to the SDGs Paul Polman, the CEO of Unilever, has said:

> Unilever is involved in the SDG agenda as we fundamentally believe these are challenges which need to be addressed for economies, businesses and society to function. We have hard-wired sustainability into everything we do across the business—our operations, innovations, our brands and our whole philosophy. There is not just a moral imperative to be sustainable but a clear business case too (Polman, 2015).

On 5 April 2016 SABMiller issued a statement on its website that it was integrating the SDGs into its sustainable development strategy. SABMiller records that it is aligning the company's existing sustainable development strategy with the SDG agenda. Anna Swaithes, the Director of Sustainable Development at SABMiller said in April 2016:

> What excites me about the SDGs is that, for the first time, the world has an agreed set of development goals which apply to every single country and every single sector. We can all find a way to coordinate effectively the delivery of the SDGs which will improve the life of every person on the planet, and also make institutions in the public sector, the private sector and civil society more successful in achieving both individual and shared objectives (quoted in Furlong, 2016).

Susanne Stormer, Vice President, Corporate Sustainability at Nova Nordisk has said the following in supporting integrated reporting:

> Our motivation for adopting <IR> was the ability to send a clear message to key audiences, investors and other stakeholders, of the way we do business and deliver value. Our stated objective was for stakeholders to enhance their valuation of the company.
>
> I see the journey of <IR> within Novo Nordisk as resembling what our business is all about: diabetes. It is chronic, progressive and irreversible.
>
> In an era of weak global economics and unstable markets, companies need to be great at telling their equity story in ways that capture how they create value for the long term. And this means information beyond what passes through the books. Since the early 1990s when our business started institutionalising what we call the Triple Bottom Line business principle, our reporting has evolved to be more fit for that purpose. With a better reporting, our business could effectively communicate

our value for the long term and carry on delivering it to the market. In our mind, <IR> is an effective tool to that end.

The centrepiece of <IR> is a clear articulation of the business model and strategy. This is perfectly compatible with our approach. We emphasise the sense of purpose and commitment that defines our business model and the way we do business. That way, our learning journey mirrors that of <IR> as a communication vehicle, through which we could reflect and drive integrated management.

Full integration of financial and non-financial information for purposes of decision-making requires parity. We created a roadmap for how to raise the equality of the social and environmental data.

Since then we have worked systematically to ensure that we have reliable data and robust internal controls in place in the same way as we do for financial data, and we are confident that when we get to the end of the 2014 reporting cycle, we will have achieved that goal. But full integration remains a goalpost and we will have much more work to do before we can call it "mission accomplished" (Tomorrow's Company, 2014, p. 19).

The benefits of integrated reporting are manifest.

12

The crucial role of accountants in creating value (and saving the planet)

The International Federation of Accountants released a document at the beginning of 2016 on the role of professional accountants in creating value with integrated thinking (IFAC, 2016). IFAC points out that integrated reporting is a process that drives organizations to focus on how to create value over time. It acknowledges that it is broader than financial reporting and that it improves organizational performance.

> Integrated thinking and reporting are significant opportunities for the more than one million professional accountants working in a variety of leadership, management, and operational roles. The opportunity is to focus on creating value for organizations and their stakeholders, as well as showing how that value is created (IFAC, 2016).

IFAC believes that integrated thinking and reporting provides an incentive for CFOs and their teams to focus on the information and decisions that matter to the organization and its potential success.

David Hodnett, Finance Director of Barclays African Group, said,

> I am accountable for reporting on the performance of the company, including the information that our executive management and board consider in decision-making. By leading the integration of performance measurements of the other capitals, the CFO is able to enhance reporting beyond just financial capital (Hodnett, 2013/14, p. 35).

What is happening today is that the CFO, with an understanding of value creation through the use of the IIRC Framework, and as a result of the mass of information both financial and non-financial available to companies, guides the board in preparing its integrated report. It is the professional CFO today that is

> contributing to an organization's efforts to sustain and create value in a broader perspective than traditional finance and accounting measures... professional accountants can be perceived as more fully meeting the needs of their employers and of society. The information and analysis they provide to support decisions needs to include a better, more expansive understanding of the disparate sources and drivers of longer-term value to enable better strategy and implementation through changes to the business model (IFAC, 2016, p. 8).

The CFOs today have long been in control of the financial aspects of a company. But the financial statements on their own are critical but not sufficient in discharging the board's duty to be accountable. A CFO who has applied his or her mind to integrated thinking and adopts the six capitals approach becomes pivotal in the whole value creation story of the company. In supporting integrated thinking the CFO takes the step in bringing about integrated reporting in the company. The CFO plays a critical role in ensuring the connection between the internal outcomes to the providers of financial capital and the external outcomes in regard to all the capitals. It will be seen that the CFOs of today are not focused only on the financial aspects of a company. They can no longer be, nor be seen to be, what for years has been called "bean counters". They have to play a pivotal role in ensuring that there is a value creation process in the company as set out in Figure 4 in Section 10 on value creation.

In the PwC (2016) survey of 1,400 CEOs in 84 countries, 82% of CEOs say that they prioritize long-term profitability over short-term and 76% say that business success is about more than just financial profit. In that context, the CFO has to add value by taking account of the interconnection and interrelationship between the inputs into a company's business model, how the company makes its money and the outcomes of how it does so. It will be seen that to describe the person who is looking across the whole value creation process as a financial officer is a misnomer. He or she should more correctly be called the chief value officer, the CVO!

13

The chief value officer

There is general acceptance today that companies operate in the triple context of the economy, society and the environment, and a board has to consider the effects of how the organization makes its money. This general acceptance is evidenced by the activism of stakeholders and especially by the activities of the responsible investment community. There are environmental shareholder activists who have, for example, launched assisted legal attacks against Exxon Mobil and have placed proposals on company proxy ballots globally, including under rules formulated by the Securities and Exchange Commission (SEC) in the USA. Many of these proposals are concerned about the resource-deprived world in which companies operate. The proposals deal with the impact of the company's business model in regard to climate change, water conservation and many sustainability issues. The response by the SEC to this activism by shareholders on the effects of a company's business model on the environment was to adopt guidelines requiring publically traded companies to make disclosures relating to climate risks.

There are now many investment houses and private equity funds that are focused on making investments in the equity of companies that are having a positive impact on society and the environment. Some of these investment houses have pointed out that assets on the balance sheets of companies could become stranded assets in a world where carbon taxation and climate change concerns are having a greater impact on business models.

An illustration of the greater value of intangible assets over tangible assets, and the need for the CEO to look at the whole value creation process, is provided by Greenpeace's attack on Nestlé over the returning of the orang-utan to its original habitat. Nestlé, the biggest food producer in the world using palm oil, was asked to assist in the reintroduction of the orang-utan to its original habitat where wetland forests had been cut down and palm oil trees grown. Nestlé was a large purchaser of that palm oil. Greenpeace produced a video of a woman buying a KitKat bar in a supermarket in Zurich (Nestlé's head office is in Geneva, Switzerland). When she opened the KitKat the severed bleeding finger of an orang-utan was in the wrapper. Nestlé obtained an injunction against the video but by then social media had spread the message far and wide. This led to negotiations that will result in the orang-utan being reintroduced into wetlands forests in its original habitat. However, the current situation is still dire for the orang-utan as it is critically endangered and threatened with imminent extinction.

When it was discovered that shoes sold by Nike had been produced by child labour in its supply chain Nike lost a large percentage of its market capitalization. The value of a company's shares is critical to the CFO because it is the currency that could be used by a company to make acquisitions rather than growing organically. There are many similar cases that have been amplified via social media and can have detrimental impacts on corporate value as well as, of course, on the humans or animals affected!

As these social and environmental factors impact so adversely on the value of that currency, it must fall within the mandate of the

CFO to ensure that nothing from how the company makes its money or what is happening in its supply chain could impact adversely on the company's market capitalization. In order to do this the CFO has to deal with the six capitals on the basis of parity, which would include taking account of the legitimate and reasonable needs, interests and expectations of the organization's major stakeholders. The CFO is therefore involved in a value creation process. He or she is no longer concerned with simply preparing the financial statements of the company according to financial reporting standards. He or she knows that the financial statements deal with only approximately 30% of the market capitalization of the company.

As value creation, rather than financial profit even at the cost of people and planet, becomes the indicator of long-term value it becomes clear that it is the professional accountant who is the most equipped of executives to lead integrated reporting in a company. Integrated thinking and reporting provides a way and an additional incentive for CFOs, and their finance teams, to focus on the information and the decisions that matter to the company and its potential success. Professional accountants as chief value officers can facilitate an understanding of value creation in a company.

While the finance function will always remain important, the role of the CFO could lose its importance if the profession does not respond to the new order.

Baruch Lev and Feng Gu (2016) argue that stakeholders are poorly served by "arcane accounting methods" and that new ways are needed to measure the company's performance. Take the example of Netflix, whose quarterly earnings announcement in April 2016, despite falling short of analysts' estimates on the announcement of their quarterly results, showed the share price increased by 80%. This was a clear indication that informed investors had not taken account of the backward-looking accounting information but rather had reacted to the forward-looking information that the number of subscribers had increased by some 900,000 more than estimated. Further, it was apparent that another reason for the earnings shortfall was that Netflix had invested heavily in technology for future growth, amounting to 99% of sales. Accountants would normally expense this in the profit and loss statement.

Backward-looking financial statements do not inform the user of the company's ability to maintain value creation in a sustainable manner. There is almost always a gap between reported earnings and share prices. It is indicative that earnings, which have always been used to predict the future performance, are no longer a reliable tool.

By focusing only on the financial statements the CFO and the user are ignoring important information about the business of the company. Without the company's long-term strategy being disclosed and showing that the sustainability issues material to the business of the company have been embedded into its strategy, the decision of investing in the equity of that company by just relying on earnings is an uninformed one. An organization where the CFO has adopted integrated thinking and treated the six capitals on a basis of parity, and has carried out the role of the professional accountant as envisaged by IFAC, will in fact be driving value creation to the long-term horizon. The user can make a much more informed assessment of the company's ability to create value in a sustainable manner.

ACCA (2013) has said that there are two strategic drivers having an impact on the role of the CFO, namely the finance function being invested with a broader remit to contribute to strategic management decisions, and "a wider concept of organisational success, broadening out from financial (profit, return on investments etc.), linked to wider social and environmental concerns".

It is clear that the accountancy profession is at a crossroads. It has to make the change to embrace that wider role by going beyond financial reporting. ACCA believes that in the education of future accountants the concept of integrated reporting should be included in the accounting curriculum.

Integrated reporting is gaining momentum internationally and it will bring about changes in the role of the finance professional. The ability to make more informed investment decisions is being achieved with integrated reports, because the board has to have spent more time understanding the financial statements and the mass of data being collected on the so-called non-financial information. Having understood the financial statements and the non-financial data collected, the board needs to extract the material information and explain it in the integrated report in clear, concise and understandable language and show how the company intends to maintain value creation in a sustainable manner.

In this scenario, the financial professional is not looking only at the financial statements or the information garnered from them. The professional has become a change-maker in looking at the six capitals on a basis of parity and taking account of the interrelationship and interconnection with the relationship between the company and its stakeholders that falls under the rubric of social capital. In this context the financial professional is a value officer rather than a financial officer. Hence he or she should be called a chief value officer – a CVO. Chief financial officer connotes that he or she is only concerned with the financial statement.

In adopting integrated reporting, a board, informed by the CVO, would give parity to the six capitals making it unnecessary to suggest that certain stakeholder groups such as workers should be represented on boards. Worker representatives on boards cannot make decisions in the best interests of the workers. They would be fettered and would be failing to discharge their legal duty to make decisions in the best interests of the company. Whatever input workers could make in the decision-making process would be covered by the board giving parity to human capital.

The role of the CVO is critical in the inclusive governance model, where a board in its decision-making process takes account of all the sources of value creation, which would include the legitimate and reasonable needs, interests and expectations of the company's material stakeholders. This clearly would include the workers, making it unnecessary to appoint a worker representative on the board.

One may well ask what about a representative of the other sources of value creation such as social, natural and intellectual capitals? These questions arise with a shareholder-centric governance model. They are irrelevant and cannot arise in adopting an inclusive stakeholder-centric governance model where parity is given to all six capitals in the board's decision-making process.

At this juncture, we thought it worth discussing a few exemplary integrated reports produced by major listed companies around the world, from a variety of industries, to show how integrated reporting is happening and how it arises from a genuine commitment to "think" in an integrated manner. There are many shining examples but we have selected a sample that gives a diversified and rich impression of how integrated reporting is working in practice. Some of the salient aspects of reporting that we considered from an integrated reporting perspective include: reporting on value creation; reporting on the six capitals; materiality decision-making; directors' remuneration and performance evaluation criteria; as well as examining the companies' approaches to sustainability and climate change mitigation.

In the finance world, South Africa's major institution *Standard Bank,* in their 2015 integrated report, asserted that: "As our primary report, our annual integrated report provides a holistic assessment of the group's ability to create value over time" (Standard Bank,

2015, p. 2). Later, they state, "… we recognise that embedding integrated thinking at every level of our organisation forms part of our longer-term work to create a culture in which risk, compliance, ethics and social responsibility are harmonised with the effective and innovative fulfilment of our clients' needs" (Standard Bank, 2015, p. 5). Within the report, the bank explains carefully how material issues are identified and emphasize that the issues considered were assessed according to commercial viability and social relevance, demonstrating an integrated approach to materiality. In relation to the six capitals, the bank explains they have not formally adopted this categorization from the IIRC's integrated reporting framework but that they allude to the company's dependence and impact on these capitals throughout their reporting. The bank clearly acknowledges the relevance of these capitals to their value creation. An especially appealing aspect of Standard Bank's report, from an integrated thinking perspective, is their adoption of "client centricity", which is defined in the report as, "placing our clients at the centre of everything we do" (Standard Bank, 2015, p. 11). In the section of their report devoted to how they create value, the bank states that they, "… manage [their] business activities and associated trade-offs, in a way that connects profitability to socially beneficial outcomes" (Standard Bank, 2015, p. 12). Also impressive is the involvement of Standard Bank in the Equator Principles, as not only does the bank follow the Principles when assessing new project finance loans of $10 million or more, but also Standard Bank was elected to chair the Equator Principles Association for 2015/16. The report also discusses the ways in which their two chief executives were evaluated and integrated thinking is in evidence in the report, with criteria including stakeholder inclusion, societal relevance, people leadership and customers, as well as financial performance. Similarly, remuneration strategy incorporates an integrated approach with additional incentive awards including financial and non-financial results.

Another exemplary integrated report comes from a completely different type of organization and context, the UK's *Crown Estate*. Their report is titled "The Crown Estate Annual Report and Accounts 2015/16: Conscious Commercialism in Action". They define "conscious commercialism" as "... being astute and enterprising in how we create value today while considering the long-term effects of what we do and how we do it" (Crown Estate, 2015/16). Further, Crown Estate emphasize that they "... consistently create significant financial value for the UK taxpayer, and tangible, long-term value, measured via our resources and relationships, for all of our stakeholders" (Crown Estate, 2015/16). The Crown Estate's approach to assessing material issues is imbued with integrated thinking as they report that they incorporate factors such as climate change and resource scarcity. The company's interim chief financial officer discussed the journey of producing integrated reports and explained the challenges of embedding genuine integrated thinking into the organisation, explaining that

> we've been embedding integrated reporting into our business planning processes and empowering employees to add value through integrating sustainable thinking into decision-making. In doing this, we have started to break down some of the silos that can occur. By thinking about business in an integrated way, we have begun to involve a more diverse range of individuals, each contributing their particular skills and knowledge" (Crown Estate, 2015/16, p. 49).

This suggests a healthy incorporation of integrated thinking into strategy and value creation, revealing a CFO who is undoubtedly a CVO.

A third illustration of integrated reporting and integrated thinking may be found in the reports of the US giant *General*

Electric. There is an informative image printed on page 25 of General Electric's Summary Integrated Report (General Electric, 2015) which provides "solutions" and bears the title "Ecomagination: Driving Real-World Solutions". The diagram includes sustainable solutions for different arms of the company, such as for Total where they state "creating hybrid cleaner energy systems for industrial use" as a focus and identify their outcome as "decreased energy costs and emissions" (General Electric, 2015). This linking of outcomes to sustainable aims is in keeping with the spirit of integrated reporting. Similarly, for Statoil, the company identifies their focus as developing "technology and techniques to increase resource efficiency and reduce emissions", with the associated outcomes as "more economical and sustainable solutions for Oil & Gas"(General Electric, 2015). Again, this shows an approach that integrates economic and environmental factors into the heart of the company's strategy.

The *Chartered Institute of Public Relations* in the UK, in their 2015 integrated report, explain how they consider "factors which may have a material impact on its ability to create and sustain value across the six capitals and to transmit value from one capital to another" (Chartered Institute of Public Relations, 2015). They, for example, identify high and moderate risks associated with financial capital and social capital. Further, the report has distinct sections devoted to discussing the different capitals, with several pages devoted to financial capital, human capital, social capital, manufactured capital, intellectual capital and environmental capital. These are then further subdivided into types such as "intellectual capital" under social capital. Indeed, the way the report is organized according to the capitals is a fine example of how integrated reporting should be "done" and how it can emerge from an approach committed to considering the capitals both separately and together.

Sanford, a New Zealand company that specializes in seafood, shows their responsible approach to marine stewardship and demonstrates integrated thinking in their second integrated annual report, which they describe as an "… integrated overview of strategy, performance and sustainable value creation" (Sanford International, 2015, p. 6). The company states that their material issues are those that relate to how Sanford creates value from their "value enablers", which they define as economic performance, people and society, sustainable raw materials, operational capability, consumers and market access. Sanford's report states, "We remain dedicated to sustainable fisheries, the environment, our people and our operations" (Sanford International, 2015, p. 17). As we discussed earlier, the United Nation's Sustainable Development Goals incorporate protection of marine biodiversity, and marine stewardship is one of the most significant challenges faced by companies, governments and NGOs in the 21st century. For a company that is completely invested in the seafood industry, ensuring proper stewardship over the oceans is critically important to their long-term value creation and survival. Unpredictable and diminishing availability and access to certain species presents a significant risk to the company's value chain, with mussels and skipjack tuna being two complex species from 100 species they fish. The report emphasizes an approach towards species that recognizes that wildlife is a natural asset which is a gift to be respected rather than a free commodity to be taken for granted. They state: "We recognise that having access to this precious resource is not a right, but a privilege. It is crucial that we treat it with respect and care. Sanford's future as a company and the long-term sustainability of the environment relies on our commitment to optimise the value of raw materials, never taking more than can be replenished" (Sanford International, 2015, p. 29). This approach is characterized by genuine sustainability, with the aim of ensuring species are available for future generations as well as protecting the marine environment through a duty of care. Sanford discuss the wide range of initiatives they are involved in ensuring the protection of the marine environment and the aquatic species therein, including performing marine mammal medical training, promoting and encouraging Fishery Improvement Projects for key species, continuing engagement with New Zealand's Deepwater Group to achieve Marine Stewardship Council (MSC) Sustainability certification for all deepwater species, and to achieve Best Aquaculture Practices Marine Farm certification to Sanford Marine Farms. These commitments demonstrate integrated thinking, as they entwine environmental sustainability and marine biodiversity protection with financial value creation and reputation enhancement. This integrated thinking is evident throughout the report in statements such as "We need to meet growing customer demand without jeopardising the marine environment for future generations" (Sanford International, 2015, p. 33).

Our last illustration comes from the South African gaming and hospitality group *Sun International*. Integrating the six capitals is at the heart of the company's 2016 report (Sun International, 2016) and they state at the beginning of the report, "Sun International appreciates that the six capitals—financial, productive, human, intellectual, social and relationship and natural capital—are all interrelated in our business to create value" (Sun International, 2016, p. 3). The company goes to great lengths to explain why their guests are core stakeholders as well as the many employees and that human and intellectual capital are critically important to value creation in their business. The elephant in the room, of course, from a social responsibility perspective, is that the company is in the gambling industry. It is therefore quite fascinating how they demonstrate commitment to ensuring gaming happens in a responsible environment and that guests are treated with respect and concern. For example they state: "Our track record of being an ethical operator and responsible corporate citizen is based on the belief that doing good is more than a business requirement, it is about creating value."

Being a responsible company in what is essentially a "sin" industry for many presents significant challenges, and the integrated report shows how the company deals with these challenges and creates value in an ethical manner. Similarly, Sun International integrates environmental issues and biodiversity into their business model, recognizing their impact on the natural environment as well as the contribution to their value creation which derives from nature: "Many of our properties are located in pristine environments rich in biodiversity, which are a key aspect of their appeal to our guests and hence we strive to protect our environments" (Sun International, 2016, p. 3).

14

Transforming the training of accountants (and saving the planet)

If we are to change the planet through the accounting function then we also have to change the accountants. This is the only way to engender real change in accounting. Unless the accountants themselves are conversant in integrated thinking, integrated reporting and their links to value creation, it is unlikely that true integrated reports will be produced. Unfortunately, the way we currently train future accountants does not adopt an integrated approach. Instead most professional training focuses on traditional financial reporting while effectively ignoring the necessary components of integrated reporting and in fact the whole new order of corporate reporting.

A salient exception to this is ACCA. ACCA has changed its training of financial officers to be value officers by placing integrated reporting within its curriculum since 2014. ACCA has said publicly "The whole concept of integrated reporting is a more lucid way to present the performance, composition, impact and contribution of the entity to stakeholders and society." It is being introduced most broadly in P1, "Governance risk and ethics" and in P2, "Corporate reporting" which are the first two compulsory papers at the professional level.

P1 addresses integrated reporting as a vehicle through which it describes the engagement, through governance structures, of the company with its responsibilities to a wider stakeholder constituency within a broader agency concept, including the impacts that the company has on its environment and how the company is responsible for a wider definition of capital than merely financial capital.

Corporate reporting in P2, the main and final level of syllabus for the ACCA qualification, will cover the whole concept of the integrated report as a broader-based approach to corporate reporting. It will give an overview of the concept in a holistic sense. The P2 examination will consider how such a report will be prepared, what it will cover and how it will increase the usefulness of the reporting function to potential users.

The training of accountants up to 2014 was focused on ensuring that the students were able to tick the boxes to obtain accreditation from a society of a certified or chartered status. Accountants should be trained today to look at the inputs into a business, how the company makes its money, how it produces its product and the effect of its product on society and the environment. This requires the educators to have a change of mind-set and to accept that it will be much more rewarding to society if the accountant can play a role as a value officer rather than merely as a financial officer. After all, the great profession of accountancy is predicated on public interest.

The usual training of accountants up till now has been in the following disciplines: accounting systems and processes; financial accounting and reporting; audit and assurance; business law; economics; finance and financial management; management accounting;

quantitative methods; taxation; information technology; and ethics. The proposed training of the accountants of tomorrow, which has started in several jurisdictions, should include the sustainability and integrated reporting aspects as now practised by ACCA. It is suggested in some jurisdictions that the student should be able to select a specialization in sustainability and/or integrated reporting. If students do not so specialize they will have a focus on the financial aspects of a company's business. This is not in the long-term interests of the profession or of sustainable development. There should also be a course on the difference between the exclusive and inclusive approaches to governance. This would include a comparison between an exclusive shareholder-centric governance model compared with an inclusive stakeholder model with the sources of value creation being considered with parity.

This change in training will enable accountants to advise on the value creation process with the outcome of sustainable capitalism.

Accountants can save the planet.

Prime Minister of the UK, Theresa May, has advocated, inter alia, a change to the shareholder governance model in the UK to a stakeholder model with long-term strategy in business and greater transparency. Integrated reporting ticks all these boxes.

Richard Kravitz, editor-in-chief of *The CPA Journal* wrote in June 2016: "By embracing sustainability initiatives, we uphold our obligation to the public, remaining relevant, vibrant, and engaged."

Based on presentations I have delivered to college students, no other subject resonates as strongly with the next generation of accounting professionals as this one. In 2014, the ACCA, in partnership with Accounting for Sustainability, undertook a study of student views on sustainability. It reported that 87% of students from 126 countries believed that accounting professionals will need to provide businesses with more decision-making insights on sustainability; 79% agreed that sustainability issues will become more important in the next 10 years; 74% agreed that environmental impact on organizations will be a bigger focus for accounting professionals; 54% wanted to be involved in integrating sustainability issues into businesses; and 34% said that the world will be a better place to live in (ACCA and A4S, 2014).

Companies are being steered by their boards down the street of last opportunity to turn away from the crisis of the planet and to move into the avenue of sustainable capitalism. The professional accountant has the most important role to play in achieving this critical outcome. That is why it is the accountant as a chief value officer who can save the planet in the 21st century.

Business persons and others, for advice on strategy and reporting turn first to their accountant before any other professional. If the accountant is able to advise organizations on integrated thinking it will result in a huge change in corporate behaviour. The CVO has a patently important role in changing corporate behaviour. Aarti Takoordeen, the CFO of the Johannesburg Stock Exchange, has said,

> In this age of dramatic distraction, disruptive new technology, increased globalisation and tough economic climate, businesses have come under serious pressure to grow whilst trending costs down. CEOs come under competitive threats like never before and are required to respond appropriately. As such they look to their finance counterparts for very different outputs compared to a few years ago. Finance professionals are no longer expected to be back office number processors, they are required to be value adding business partners.

The curriculums at tertiary institutions need to change to include the sustainability and integrated reporting areas set out above. Accountants who have not had the benefit of that changed curriculum should have training through their accountancy bodies about the value creation process.

The AICPA and the CIMA are merging and their professional qualifications will become known as Chartered Global Management Accountant (CGMA). Their current leaders, Barry Melancon (President and CEO, AICPA) and Charles Tilley (Chief Executive, CIMA), have for years been supporting integrated thinking. Both will play senior roles in CGMA. Barry Melancon is the Chairman of the IIRC's Operating Company and Charles Tilley sits on the board as an adviser. He played a critical role in finalising the IIRC's Framework of 2013 (IIRC, 2013). They are determined that the combined CGMA membership of 620,000 will be imbued with a knowledge of integrated reporting. These members, spread throughout the world, will be in a position to advise their clients on the development of strategy treating the six capitals on a basis of parity which will include taking account of the legitimate and reasonable needs, interests and expectations of the company's stakeholders. They will ensure that the sustainability issues material to the business of the company are embedded into the company's strategy. The outcome for the companies that CGMAs will advise will be the achievement of sustainable capitalism.

Amir Dossal, a chartered accountant and a member of the Institute of Chartered Accountants in England and Wales, has 25 years of distinguished service with the United Nations dealing with economic and social issues. In a recent interview about the role of the accountancy profession he said,

> Accountants are critical because they can demonstrate the value driven approach of smart philanthropy and social investment. It is a timing difference—instead of saying I am working for Wall Street and tomorrow's results, the City should be asking about long-term sustainability measures. We need results measured on that basis and not short-term performance. Accountants can extrapolate that and make it clear cut (Cree, 2016).

No CFOs today can, with justification, contend that the financial statements can determine value creation in a company. If they did so, they would be ignoring red flashing lights, because it has clearly been shown that at least 70% of the market cap of major companies is made up of intangible assets that are not additives in a balance sheet according to financial reporting standards. It will lead to uninformed decision-making by a board and a lack of engagement with key stakeholders, with the consequent increased risk of failure.

Concluding discussion and recommendations

This book addresses corporate governance, corporate reporting and issues of sustainability from new perspectives. Taking age-old concepts such as "agency theory" and "shareholder ownership", the discussion and arguments herein show how they have become outdated and largely irrelevant in today's business environment. Shareholders have responsibility and power but they are not the "real" owners of a company. A company requires the board and its stakeholders to take responsibility for the corporate entity, which is incapacitated and has no "power" of its own. In a changing world, at a critical tipping point because of climate change, global warming, growing poverty and wealth inequalities, drought, famine and concerns for species extinction, it is no longer appropriate for businesses to concern themselves solely with "shareholder wealth maximization" and maximizing corporate profits at the expense of our natural environment, workers' rights and protection, care for suppliers, health and safety, and concerns for other species as well as ourselves. Proper engagement with a company's stakeholders needs to encourage fair and equal dialogue. The introduction of a corporate stakeholder relationship officer into companies should facilitate enhanced stakeholder relations as well as lead to enhanced corporate value. Only through effective, inclusive dialogue can stakeholder concerns be adequately addressed and companies be aware of, and understand, these concerns. Considering stakeholder interests in an inclusive manner is critical to building corporate reputation as well as maintaining and enhancing corporate value in today's world.

Following traditional finance theory and pursuing shareholder value on a short-term basis, with consideration only for financially driven short-term returns will only lead to complete disaster in coming decades. Even the concept of "enlightened shareholder value", which takes environmental, social and governance factors into account, to the extent that they are relevant to financial value, is insufficient to "save the planet". The training of accountants (and others in the finance industry) needs to incorporate issues of sustainability, climate change and carbon accounting, reporting on greenhouse gas emissions, and extinction accounting. Integrated reporting provides a solution to all of these problems. The integrated report is an ideal vehicle for companies to report on all relevant and material social, environmental and economic issues which affect and are affected by the company's operations. The evolution of integrated thinking is essential if companies are to embrace genuine stakeholder accountability and ultimately save the planet. Integrated reporting provides the ideal "home" for information and disclosures relating to Sustainable Development Goals, the GRI Principles, the six capitals, the Sustainability Accounting Standards Board standards, and a company's attempts to prevent species extinction. Introducing the concept of the Chief Value Officer, enhances a company's efforts to maximize corporate value across all six capitals and provides a means for accountants to "save the planet". A Chief Value Officer can ensure a company navigates through the diverse, dangerous, opaque, complex, multi-layered, multifaceted, kaleidoscopic world of the 21st century.

References

ACCA (Association of Chartered Certified Accountants) (2013). *Accountants and Strategic Leadership*. Retrieved from http://www.accaglobal.com/content/dam/acca/global/PDF-technical/other-PDFs/Accountants-Strategic-Leadership.pdf.

ACCA & A4S (Association of Chartered Certified Accountants & Accounting for Sustainability) (2014). *Sustainability and Business: The Next Ten Years. ACCA Students' Views on Sustainability*. Retrieved from http://www.accaglobal.com/content/dam/acca/global/PDF-technical/sustainability-reporting/presentation-sustainability-and-business-the-next-10-years.pdf.

ASSC (Accounting Standards Steering Committee) (1975). *The Corporate Report*. London: Author.

Atkins, J.F., & Atkins, B. (Eds.) (2016). *The Business of Bees: An Integrated Approach to Bee Decline and Corporate Responsibility,* Sheffield, UK: Greenleaf.

Atkins, J.F., & Atkins, B. (eds.) (forthcoming). *Around the World in 80 Species: Exploring the Business of Extinction,* Sheffield, UK: Greenleaf.

Atkins, J.F., & Maroun, W. (2014). *South African Institutional Investors' Perceptions of Integrated Reporting*. London: Association of Chartered Certified Accountants.

Atkins, J.F., Gräbsch, C., & Jones, M.J. (2014). Biodiversity reporting: Exploring its anthropocentric nature. In M.J. Jones (Ed.) *Accounting for Biodiversity*. Abingdon, UK: Routledge.

Atkins, J.F., Maroun, W., Barone, E., & Atkins, B.C. (2015). From the Big Five to the Big Four? Exploring Extinction Accounting for the Rhinoceros? Paper presented at University of Dundee's Staff Seminar Series in September 2015. (Currently under second review for publication in *Accounting, Auditing & Accountability Journal*.)

Atkinson, G., & D. Pearce (1995). Measuring sustainable development. In D.W. Bromley (Ed.), *Handbook of Environmental Economics* (pp. 166-182). Oxford, UK: Blackwell.

Barone, E., Ranamagar, N., & Solomon, J.F. (2013). A Habermasian model of stakeholder (non)engagement and corporate (ir)responsibility reporting. *Accounting Forum, 37 (3), pp. 163-181.*

Berle, A., & Means, G. (1932). *The Modern Corporation and Private Property*. New York: Transaction Publishers.

Butler, S., & Kollewe, J. (2016, 25 August). More shareholders criticise Sports Direct's corporate governance: L&G and Aberdeen Asset Management join Investor Forum in calling for plan of action to rebuild confidence in retailer. *The Guardian online.*

Camfferman, K., & Zeff, S. (2003). The apotheosis of holding company accounting: Unilever's financial reporting innovations from the 1920s to the 1940s. Accounting, Business & Financial History, 13 (2), pp. 171-206.

Carl. D.M., & Nguyen, H. (2012, 23 March). California Benefit Corporations: Installing a corporate conscience. Interview with John Montgomery. *UC Davis Business Law Journal*. Retrieved from http://blj.ucdavis.edu/archives/vol-11-no-1/interview-john-montgomery.html

Carney, Mark (2015, 29 September). Breaking the tragedy of the horizon: Climate change and financial stability. Speech given at Lloyd's of London.

Chartered Institute of Public Relations (2015). *Integrated Report 2015*. United Kingdom. Retrieved from: https://www.cipr.co.uk/sites/default/files/Final%20interactive%20IR%202015.pdf

CIMA (Chartered Institute of Management Accountants), IFAC (International Federation of Accountants), EY & Natural Capital Coalition (2014). *Accounting for Natural Capital: The Elephant in the Boardroom*, London: Chartered Institute of Management Accountants.

Collison, D., Cross, S., Ferguson, J., Power, D., & Stevenson, L. (2011). *Shareholder Primacy in UK Corporate Law: An Exploration of the Rationale and Evidence, ACCA Research Report 125*. London: Certified Accountants Educational Trust.

Corporate Governance Committee (1992). *Report of the Committee on the Financial Aspects of Corporate Governance: The Code of Best Practice* (known as the Cadbury Report). London: Gee Professional Publishing.

Cree, R. (2016, 2 March). Amir Dossal: History man, Economia. Retrieved from http://economia.icaew.com/people/march-2016/amir-dossal-winner-of-icaews-outstanding-achievement-award

Crown Estate (2015/16). *The Crown Estate Annual Report*. United Kingdom. Retrieved from: https://www.gov.uk/government/uploads/system/uploads/attachment_data/file/537945/crown_estate_annual_report_.pdf

Department of Trade and Industry (2002), *Modernising Company Law White Paper presented to Parliament, by the Secretary of State for Trade and Industry July 2002*. London: The Stationery Office.

Eccles, R.G., & Krzus, M.P. (2010). *One Report: Integrated Reporting for a Sustainable Strategy*, Hoboken, New Jersey: John Wiley.

Freeman, E. (1984). *Strategic Management: A Stakeholder Approach*. Boston, MA: Pitman Press.

Friedman, M. (1970, 13 September). The social responsibility of business is to increase its profits, *New York Times Magazine*, (Reprinted in T.L. Beauchamp & N. Bowie (1988). *Ethical Theory and Business*, Englewood Cliffs, NJ: Prentice Hall, pp. 87–91).

Furlong, H. (2016, 1 July). How SABMiller is furthering the SDGs to help the world "prosper". *Sustainable Brands*. Retrieved from http://www.sustainablebrands.com/news_and_views/brand_innovation/hannah_furlong/how_sabmiller_furthering_sdgs_help_world_prosper.

Gallhofer, S., & Haslam, J. (2003). *Accounting and Emancipation: Some Critical Interventions*. London: Routledge.

Gallhofer, S., Haslam, J., & Yonekura, A. (2015). Accounting as differentiated universal for emancipatory praxis. *Accounting, Auditing & Accountability Journal*, 28(5), pp. 846-874.

General Electric (2015). *Summary Integrated Report*. United States. Retrieved from: https://www.ge.com/ar2015/assets/pdf/GE_AR15_Integrated_Summary_Report.pdf

Global Sustain (2015, 3 August). Sri Lanka latest country to see economic benefit of Integrated Reporting Retrieved from http://globalsustain.org/en/story/10647.

Goedhart, M., Koller, T., & Wessels, D. (2015, March). *The real business of business is business*. McKinsey & Co. Retrieved from http://www.mckinsey.com/business-functions/strategy-and-corporate-finance/our-insights/the-real-business-of-business.

Guthrie, L. (2016). *Mapping the Sustainability Reporting Landscape: Lost in the Right Direction*. London: Association of Chartered Certified Accountants and Climate Disclosure Standards Board.

Habermas, J. (2001). *On the Pragmatics of Social Interaction: Preliminary Studies in the Theory of Communicative Action* (B. Fultner, Trans.), Cambridge, UK: Polity Press. (Original work published 1984).

Haldane, A. (2015). Who owns a company? Speech given at University of Edinburgh Corporate Finance Conference, 22 May 2015. Retrieved from http://www.bankofengland.co.uk/publications/Pages/speeches/2015/833.aspx.

Haldane, A. (2016). The great divide. Speech given at New City Agenda Annual Dinner, 18 May 2016. Retrieved from http://www.bankofengland.co.uk/publications/Documents/speeches/2016/speech908.pdf.

Hayhow, D.B, Burns, F., Eaton, M.A., Al Fulaij, N., August, T.A., Babey, L., ... Gregory, R.D. (2016). *State of Nature 2016*. Sandy, UK: The State of Nature Partnership

Hebb, T., Hawley, J., Hoepner, A., Neher, A. & Wood, D. (2015). *The Routledge Companion to Responsible Investment*. Abingdon, UK: Routledge.

Hodnett, D. (2013/14). Integrated Reporting: The role of the CFO. *Accountancy SA*, Dec. 13/Jan.14.

ICGN (International Corporate Governance Network) (2014) *Global Governance Principles* (4th ed.). London: Author.

IFAC (International Federation of Accountants) (2016). *Creating Value with Integrated Thinking: The Role of Professional Accountants*, New York: Author. Retrieved from https://www.ifac.org/publications-resources/creating-value-integrated-thinking.

IFAC (International Federation of Accountants), CIMA (Chartered Institute of Management Accountants), & PwC (2013). *Business Model: Background Paper for <IR>*. International Integrated Reporting Council. Retrieved from integratedreporting.org/wp-content/uploads/2013/03/Business_Model.pdf.

Institute of Directors in Southern Africa (2011). *CRISA: Code for Responsible Investing in South Africa*. Johannesburg: Author.

IIRC (International Integrated Reporting Council) (2013). *The International <IR> Framework*. Retrieved from http://integratedreporting.org/wp-content/uploads/2013/12/13-12-08-THE-INTERNATIONAL-IR-FRAMEWORK-2-1.pdf.

Jansson, A., Hammer, M., Folke, C., & Costanza, R. (Eds.) (1994). *Investing in Natural Capital: The Ecological Economics Approach to Sustainability*. Washington, DC: Island Press.

Jensen, M.C., & Meckling, W.H. (1976). Theory of the firm: Managerial behaviour, agency costs and ownership structure. *Journal of Financial Economics*, 3, pp. 305-360.

Jones, M.J., & Solomon, J.F. (2013). Problematising accounting for biodiversity. *Accounting, Auditing & Accountability Journal*, 26(5), pp. 668-687.

King Committee on Corporate Governance (King I) (1994). *The King Report on Corporate Governance*. Parktown, South Africa: Institute of Directors in Southern Africa.

King Committee on Corporate Governance (King II) (2002). *The King Report on Corporate Governance for South Africa*. Parktown, South Africa: Institute of Directors in Southern Africa.

King Committee on Corporate Governance (King III) (2009). *King Report on Governance for South Africa*. Parktown, South Africa: Institute of Directors in Southern Africa.

KPMG (2011). *KPMG International Survey of Corporate Responsibility Reporting*. Amstelveen, Netherlands: KPMG International.

Lev, B., & Gu, F. (2016). *The End of Accounting and the Path Forward for Investors and Managers*. Hoboken, NJ: Wiley.

Natural Capital Coalition (2016). *Natural Capital Protocol* . Retrieved from www.naturalcapitalcoalition.org/protocol.

Peters, S., & Allen, J. (2016, 10 February). Investors too need to be more rigorous [Letter]. *The Financial Times*.

Polman, P. (2015, 21 September). Paul Polman interview with Business Green, transcript, Unilever, https://www.unilever.com/news/speeches/Paul-Polman-interview-with-Business-Green.html

Porter, M., & Kramer, M.R. (2011). Creating shared value. *Harvard Business Review*, 89 (1/2), pp. 62-77.

PwC (2016). PwC's 19th Annual Global CEO Survey: What's on the minds of over 1,400 CEOs around the world?. Retrieved from http://www.pwc.com/gx/en/ceo-agenda/ceosurvey/2016.html.

Ross, S. (1973). The economic theory of agency: The principal's problem. *American Economic Review*, 63, pp. 134-139.

Sanford International (2015). *Salt in Our Veins: Sanford Annual Report*. New Zealand. Retrieved from: http://www.sanford.co.nz/assets/announcements/SAN044-AR-2015-WEB_spreads.pdf

Sikka, P. (2016). Debunking the myth of shareholder ownership of companies, paper presented at the third GARI conference, Henley Centre for Governance, Accountability & Responsible Investment, Henley Business School, 18–20 April 2016.

Solomon, J. (2013). *Corporate Governance and Accountability* (4th ed.). John Wiley & Sons.

Standard Bank (2015). *Annual Integrated Report*. South Africa. Retrieved from: http://reporting.standardbank.com/downloads/SBG_FY15_Annual%20integrated%20report.pdf

Sun International (2016). 2016 *Integrated Annual Report*. South Africa. Retrieved from: http://suninternational.onlinereport.co.za

Tomorrow's Company (2014). *Tomorrow's Business Success: Using Integrated Reporting to Help Create Value and Effectively Tell the Full Story*. Commissioned and cofunded by CIMA and the IIRC, London: Centre for Tomorrow's Company.

Turner, M. (2016, 2 February). Here is the letter the world's largest investor, BlackRock CEO Larry Fink, just sent to CEOs everywhere, *Business Insider UK*. Retrieved from http://uk.businessinsider.com/blackrock-ceo-larry-fink-letter-to-sp-500-ceos-2016-2.

UN (2015). *Outcome Document of the Third International Conference on Financing for Development (FfD3) Addis Ababa Agenda Action*, 13-16 July 2015. Retrieved from http://www.un.org/ga/search/view_doc.asp?symbol=A/CONF.227/L.1.

UN, Department of Economic and Social Affairs (2015). *World Population Prospects: The 2015 Revision*. New York: United Nations.

Walker Review (2009). *A Review of Corporate Governance in UK Banks and Other Financial Industry Entities: Final Recommendations*. London: Walker Review Secretariat.

About the authors

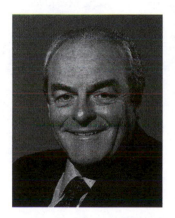

Mervyn King is a Senior Counsel and former Judge of the Supreme Court of South Africa. He is Professor Extraordinaire at the University of South Africa on Corporate Citizenship, Honorary Professor at the Universities of Pretoria and Cape Town and a Visiting Professor at Rhodes.

He has an honorary Doctorate of Laws from the Universities of the Witwatersrand and Leeds, is Chairman of the King Committee on Corporate Governance in South Africa, which produced King I, II and III, and is First Vice President of the Institute of Directors Southern Africa. He is Chairman of the International Integrated Reporting Council (IIRC), Chairman Emeritus of the Global Reporting Initiative (GRI) and a member of the Private Sector Advisory Group to the World Bank on Corporate Governance. He chaired the United Nations Committee on Governance and Oversight and was President of the Advertising Standards Authority for 15 years.

Mervyn has been a chairman, director and chief executive of several companies listed on the London, Luxembourg and Johannesburg Stock Exchanges. He has consulted, advised and spoken on legal, business, advertising, sustainability and corporate governance issues in over 60 countries and has received many awards from international bodies around the world. He is the author of three books on governance, sustainability and reporting and sits as an arbitrator and mediator internationally.

Jill Atkins holds a Chair in Financial Management at Sheffield University Management School, the University of Sheffield, and is also a visiting professor at the University of the Witwatersrand, South Africa. She previously worked as a professor at Henley Business School and King's College London.

Her research focuses on several areas including responsible investment, stakeholder accountability, social accounting, integrated reporting and corporate governance. Jill chairs the British Accounting & Finance Association's Special Interest Group on Corporate Governance and enjoys organizing conferences that bring together governance specialists from the academia, corporate and investor communities.